# The GOD We WORSHIP

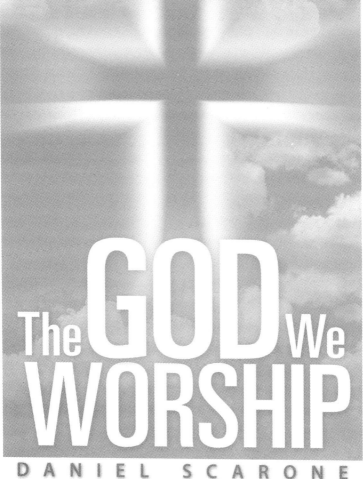

# WHAT THE BIBLE SAYS ABOUT

# The GOD We WORSHIP

## DANIEL SCARONE

**Pacific Press® Publishing Association**
Nampa, Idaho
Oshawa, Ontario, Canada
www.pacificpress.com

Cover design by Pacific Press® Publishing Association
Cover design resources from Click Graphic Design © 2011
Inside design by Aaron Troia

Copyright © 2011 by Pacific Press® Publishing Association
Printed in the United States of America
All rights reserved

The author assumes full responsibility for the accuracy of all facts and quotations as cited in this book.

Unless otherwise indicated, Scripture quotations are taken from the King James Version.

Scripture quotations marked ESV are from The Holy Bible, English Standard Version® (ESV®), copyright © 2001 by Crossway, a publishing ministry of Good News Publishers. Used by permission. All rights reserved.

Scripture marked ISV is taken from the Holy Bible: International Standard Version®. Copyright © 1996–2008 by The ISV Foundation. All rights reserved internationally. Used by permission.

Scriptures quoted from NASB are from *The New American Standard Bible*®, Copyright © 1960, 1962, 1963, 1968, 1971, 1972, 1973, 1975, 1977, 1995 by The Lockman Foundation. Used by permission.

Scripture quotations marked NIV are from The Holy Bible, NEW INTERNATIONAL VERSION®. Copyright © 1973, 1978, 1984, 2011 by Biblica, Inc. Used by permission. All rights reserved worldwide.

Scriptures quoted from NKJV are from The New King James Version, copyright © 1979, 1980, 1982, Thomas Nelson, Inc., Publishers.

Scripture quotations marked NLT are taken from the Holy Bible, New Living Translation, copyright © 1996, 2004, 2007. Used by permission of Tyndale House Publishers, Inc., Wheaton, Illinois 60189. All rights reserved.

Scripture texts credited to NRSV are from the New Revised Standard Version of the Bible, copyright © 1989 by the Division of Christian Education of the National Council of the Churches of Christ in the USA. Used by permission. All rights reserved.

Scripture quotations from the *New World Translation of the Holy Scriptures,* copyright © 1961, 1981, 1984 Watch Tower Bible and Tract Society of Pennsylvania and International Bible Students Association. All rights reserved.

You can obtain additional copies of this book by calling toll-free 1-800-765-6955 or by visiting http://www.adventistbookcenter.com.

Library of Congress Cataloging-in-Publication Data:

ISBN 13: 978-0-8163-2517-7
ISBN 10: 0-8163-2517-0

12 13 14 15 • 5 4 3 2

# Acknowledgments

I would like to express my sincere and deep appreciation to several people who took the time to review the material that composes this small document and who kindly gave me their advice: Professor Mike Lynch, who reviewed the manuscript and greatly improved its English; Tennille Shin, who did the first edit of the manuscript; Elder Loren Nelson, who did a second edit; Elder Jay Gallimore and Elder Jim Micheff, for their invaluable coaching and suggestions; Elder Ron du Preez, for taking time to review the theological scenario of the book; and Elder Luis Eguiluz, for his proofreading.

I mustn't forget to express my gratitude also to my son Rene D. Scarone for his suggestions, and to Lira, my wife, because she has always been willing to help me find important bibliographical sources.

And I want to express my gratitude to God, who gave me life and has permitted me to write about Him.

# Contents

# Preface

*The God We Worship* aims to help modern readers understand God's disclosures of Himself in Scripture.

Ancient Bible writers, early Christian apostles, and subsequent generations of translators all faced great challenges as they attempted to communicate the things God wants to share with humanity. Difficult as was their task, though, they thrilled to the spiritual discoveries they made day by day as their work progressed.

A similar experience will be ours as we seek answers to the many questions that come to mind as we read the Word of God. None of us will ever fully master the divine science, but God's unfolding gift permits us continually more rewarding glimpses of His Person as portrayed in His Word. Inspiration and worship—the life blood of the church—center on that revelation. In daily meditations and Sabbath convocations, we believers are invited into the awesome Presence so we can render to Him ever more knowledgeable recognition. It is my prayer that this book will reinforce faith in God and safeguard against distractions that becloud the scriptural image of Him.

In this study, we will explore what the Bible tells us about this God whom we worship. Who is He? What does Scripture say about His person? How shall we understand this God who is enthroned as the very center of all our worship?

My primary purpose in writing this book is to address some views regarding the tri-unity of God—in other words, the Trinity—that are being adopted by some of the rank and file members of the Seventh-day Adventist Church. The doctrine of God we hold and teach is coming under questioning from various directions. Too often, those doing the questioning haven't followed the biblical model of bringing the matter to the church and working up through the system—an approach that would draw sound biblical scrutiny all along the way. Instead, the challenges to this doctrine of ours have been spread through e-mails, Web sites, video clips, self-published books and pamphlets, and so forth. Some of these presentations are straightforward and direct; but generally, they are indirect and even rather subtle.

The title I have chosen for this little book, *The God We Worship,* is intended to set the stage for the theology and Christian reflection found in its pages. We have no pantheon of gods; our God is One. He is also unique, standing apart from all other so-called gods. All our adoration is focused on Him. From Sabbath to Sabbath we gather to worship and adore Him as the Creator of our world and of the entire universe.

"Now unto the King eternal, immortal, invisible, the only wise God, be honour and glory for ever and ever. Amen" (1 Timothy 1:17). With reverence in our hearts, let's talk about Him.

# Chapter 1
# Why a Book About God?

Reflecting on God—on who and what God is—is a sacred task. The doctrine of God is foundational to the Bible. In essence, the Bible remains authoritative only if we maintain its central teaching—what it says about God. And in turn, what Christian churches believe about God shapes every other belief of doctrine that they hold. What we believe about God affects our view of

- Creation,
- who we are, since we're made in the image of God,
- the memorial rest on the seventh day, the biblical Sabbath,
- the institution of marriage and the family,
- the appearance of sin,
- the doctrine of restoration implemented by God to save humans from sin,
- the teaching of the revelation and inspiration of Scripture,
- the choosing of God's people,
- the Exodus and the Promised Land,
- the Ten Commandments,
- the notion of God's law,
- patriarchs, prophets, and priests,
- what the sanctuary and its services teach,
- the meaning of time prophecies,
- the Messiah and His coming,
- Jesus' virgin birth,

- His ministry,
- His teachings,
- the Lord's Supper,
- His substitutionary death,
- His resurrection and ascension into heaven,
- the Holy Spirit,
- the selection of disciples,
- the New Testament writings,
- the idea of a church,
- the practice of baptism,
- the second coming of Jesus,
- eternal life, and on and on.

Think about it!

The notion of God undergirds the values of nations. Without it, the Western worldview and all of its values would vanish. One example of this is the Pledge of Allegiance of the United States of America: "I pledge allegiance to the flag of the United States of America, and to the republic for which it stands, one nation under God, indivisible, with liberty and justice for all."

No question about it, the doctrine of God is vitally important.

## Hebrew and Greek reflection

The story of salvation has had an interesting trip through history, adapting along the way to different time periods and varying civilizations, cultures, and languages. Modern Bible readers sometimes bounce back and forth between the Old and New Testaments without realizing that more than four centuries separate them. During those transitional years, radically important changes were taking place that affected the then-known world in geopolitical, social, religious, and linguistic fashion, drawing together in ways never before seen a cosmopolitan cross section of humanity.

A very important historical phenomenon, all too often disregarded by the uninformed, transpired during those intertestamental years—the Hellenization of the Mediterranean world and the Middle East. The political dominance of Greece, though of short duration, left a cultural mark that proved itself to be practically timeless. This influential development brought critical changes in politics, culture, and language to a major portion of both the Western world and the Middle East.

The Old Testament was written mostly in Hebrew, with a smattering of Aramaic, while all of the New Testament was written in Greek. The Old Testament was overwhelmingly Hebrew in culture and language, while, for the most part, the New Testament was written in Greek by authors saturated with a Jewish culture determined to survive in a Latin-dominated world.

Even when Hebrews and Greeks share concepts, they think about them in different ways. In order to understand some very crucial ideas, we need to take these differences into account. Let's consider some of them in relation to the doctrine of God:

1. *Concerning the existence of God:* Greeks try to *prove* His existence. Hebrews *assume* His existence.
2. *Concerning our understanding of God:* Greeks focus on His *being*. Hebrews focus on His *relationships*.
3. *Concerning faith in God:* Greeks see faith as *intellectual;*

they express it through creeds and doctrines. Hebrews see faith as *relational* and *personal;* they express it in terms of relationship rather than as a mental construct.[1]

All of these elements are critical to our understanding of
this doctrine of God. Taking that into account, this book
aims to provide an approach to God from the perspective of
how *He* decided to reveal Himself in Scripture.

Of course, we also need to take into account some elements that proved troublesome in history and led to be-
trayal, with some exceedingly unfortunate consequences for
the understanding of many Bible topics.

## The great historical disengagement

Down through the centuries the Christian
church has faced a variety of risks. Very early on the
Christian movement lost its home base in Jerusalem
(70 AD) and its umbilical cord of closely embedded
history with Judaism was severed. Subsequent generations of church leaders lost the Hebrew tongue
and gave diminishing importance to the Old Testament as formative Scripture for Christianity. Addi-
tionally, they lost sight of the continuing validity of
the Ten Commandments, dropped the Sabbath as a
memorial of Creation, and the Christian church
wandered away from the concept of discipleship. As
the centuries rolled on, the church blended increas-
ingly into the ways of the world.[2]

In a relatively brief time, the Christian church outgrew

its original Jewish matrix and became transformed into a predominantly Gentile phenomenon. As that process of historical disruption unfolded, a clear distinction developed between the earlier, or apostolic, and the subsequent, or subapostolic, stage of Christian history. During the years immediately following the ascension of Christ, the original disciples and their converts in the Jewish homeland naturally felt the ties of continuation to the faith of their forebearers. That most likely seemed all the more reasonable to them as they recalled the words of the Messiah, who declared that His purpose in coming to earth was not to "destroy the law, or the prophets . . . but to fulfil" them (Matthew 5:17, 18).

The destruction of Jerusalem and its great Jewish temple in A.D. 70 serves historians as a convenient event with which to mark as the point at which Jewish and Gentile Christians within the early church's growing population began to go their separate ways. As the first century advanced, an in-house conflict arose between Hellenistic Jews and Hellenistic Jewish Christians; the swelling numbers of Gentile Christians, bringing along with them pagan Hellenistic baggage, added another disruptive element. It can be argued that the evolving church was becoming a hodge-podge of ingredients that was losing what had once been the heart of its historical and scriptural heritage.

Jaroslav Pelikan, a scholar of the history of Christianity, wrote,

> The relations of the church fathers to Judaism
> and to pagan thought affected much of what they
> had to say about the various doctrinal issues before

them. The development of the doctrine of the person of Jesus Christ in relation to the Father must be studied largely on the basis of writings drafted against heresy, against Judaism, and against paganism. In the case of most of the so-called apologists, only writings of these kinds have survived, even though we know that some of them wrote other books addressed specifically to their fellow Christians.[3]

Pelikan indicates that this postapostolic, post–New Testament church survived, but its theologians had to structure their faith as a bulwark against Christian heresy, Judaism, and paganism. Because no one had yet written a formal statement of their beliefs, "we must therefore attempt to determine what they were believing and teaching on the basis of what they confessed."[4]

## Effects of the disengagement

"According to tradition, only one of the writers of the New Testament, Luke, was not a Jew." As far as it is known, none of the subapostolic church fathers were Jews. Justin Martyr was born in Samaria, and for that reason he was considered a Gentile.[5]

The Christian church began to separate itself from its Hebrew roots quite early on. Pelikan reminds us that the second-century church fathers neither read nor spoke Hebrew, a fact clearly revealing a degree of isolation from the Scriptures that had served the original church in the time of Christ and His disciples. Obviously, this disconnect widened as thousands of new Gentile converts from paganism, people who had no ties to Judaism, joined the church. From among their ranks rose new church leaders whose voices would be heard with authority, and those voices were influenced by the Greek pagan milieu from which they sprang. In consequence, the Old Testament—and especially, its first five books, the Law—lost its authority as the judge of their writings. So, the evolving church took on a new identity, a kind of hybridization of paganism, Platonism, and traditional Christianity. Eventually, the Roman Catholic Church grew out of this new body.

In the course of time, all church doctrine became defined in carefully worded fashion. The process of discussing and shaping these doctrines took place under the umbrella of ecumenical councils, which, at that time, were influenced by leaders whose Greek mentality made it difficult for them to capture on paper the teachings of the early Christian church that had grown out of the thought and language of the Hebrews. During those early church synods and councils, theologians influenced by Greek thought, which was their heritage and culture, hammered out the formulas by which the church would view and define God's personhood. The hierarchical order and the priorities of rank within the Godhead were defined by phrases that conformed to statements of that which the church thought to be proper for defining universal belief. As a consequence, God was squeezed into word images limited by their human origin. Battles over the Greek terms and philosophical nuances, coupled with pride, politics, and often bitter emotions, resulted in more heat than light regarding the Father, the Son, and the Holy Spirit, thus jeopardizing the pure doctrine that God had revealed about Himself.

There is no evidence that such problems as these arose among those whose thinking grew out of the Hebrew culture. For them, understanding the Godhead was a simple matter of accepting God just as He reveals Himself in Scripture. But what was natural to the Hebrew mind seemed unnatural to the Greek mind, which was oriented to analysis and conjecture. Leaving the concept of God free from these overwrought mental gymnastics protected it from the kinds of distortions that would come to be seen later, when Greek minds replaced the Hebrew sages.

The doctrine of God exercises a powerful influence on all of our fundamental beliefs. As Christ's church in our time and the remnant of the Lord at the time of the end, we need to be united in our vision of the God we worship. Professor Raoul Dederen, a specialist in systematic theology and former dean of the seminary at Andrews University, recognized the importance for modern-day Christians to possess an understanding of the doctrine of the Godhead that is both sound and clear. He wrote,

> To a large number of Christians . . . [the doctrine of the Trinity] is a doctrine fundamental to Christianity since it deals with a correct knowledge of God. Related to the divine Being, his nature and mode of being, this knowledge affects every man's understanding of God as the object of his worship, whether he regards him as one in essence and one in person, or admits that in the unity of the Deity there are three equally divine persons. It cannot be an irrelevant subject. If the doctrine of the Trinity is true, then those who deny it do not worship the God of

the Scriptures. If it is false, the Trinitarians, by paying divine honor to the Son and to the Holy Spirit, are equally guilty of idolatry. The doctrine of the Trinity is not merely speculation, but lies at the root of every man's theology and affects the whole creed and practice.[6]

1. See "Think Hebrew" Follow the Rabbi, http://www.followtherabbi .com/Brix?pageID=1854 for more information.

2. Daniel Scarone, "Why Are General Conferences Sessions Held?" Adventist Pastor Online, accessed May 18, 2011, http:// www.adventistpastoronline.com/index.php/why-are-general-conference-sessions-held/.

3. Jaroslav Pelikan, *The Christian Tradition: A History of the Development of Doctrine,* vol. 1, *The Emergence of the Catholic Tradition (100-600)* (Chicago: University of Chicago Press, 1975), 11.

4. Ibid., 11.

5. Ibid., 12.

6. Raoul Dederen, "Reflections on the Doctrine of the Trinity," *Andrews University Seminary Studies* 8, no. 1 (January 1970 ): 1, 2.

# Chapter 2
# Tri-unity in the Old Testament

When I was a young theology major in college in Argentina, I accepted an invitation to present a talk about the Bible to patients and visitors at River Plate Sanatorium.[1] At the conclusion, a fellow student came up to tell me that one of the patients wanted me to visit him and explain more about God. My friend added, "Keep in mind that he is Jewish."

That didn't present any insurmountable difficulties; after all, the early Christian believers were also Jewish. When Paul declared that "all Scripture is given by inspiration of God" (2 Timothy 3:16), it's obvious that the Scripture he was writing about was the Old Testament because the New Testament had not yet been written. So, this Jewish man and I could find ample common ground studying together from the Old Testament.

I chose to go directly to the root of the matter with my new acquaintance by focusing on the fundamental article of faith among the children of Israel, the *Sh'ma:* "Hear, O Israel: The LORD our God is one LORD" (Deuteronomy 6:4; this passage is known as the *Sh'ma* because it begins with the verb "hear," *sh'ma*). Moses instructed the Israelites to repeat this statement of belief every morning and again every evening.

The *Sh'ma* contains several items of interest: the number of times the name of God is mentioned, the use of the term *Elohim,* and the use of *echad* at the end of the verse. The *Sh'ma* refers to God three times: "Hear, O Israel: The LORD

[*YHWH;* first mention] our God [*Elohenu;* second mention], the Lᴏʀᴅ [*YHWH;* third mention] is one!" (NKJV). The writers of the Old Testament use several names for God, but probably the names used most frequently are "Lᴏʀᴅ" (*YHWH*) and "God" (*Elohim**). The name *YHWH* is also known as the Tetragrammaton, or "the four letters." It's the name of God used most frequently in the Old Testament.†

## The use of *Elohim*

The second item in Deuteronomy 6:4 that has significance for our study is the word *Elohim*—a word that is used 2,602 times in Scripture.‡ *Elohim* is the plural form of the word *El* (God). Since it is the plural form of that word, naturally, it has connotations of plurality. In fact, in the first commandment, this word is explicitly plural: "Thou shalt have no other gods before me" (Exodus 20:3). The Hebrew word that is translated "gods" is *Elohim.*

In contrast with verse 3, verse 1 reads, "And God spake all these words, saying." In the Hebrew original, the word translated "God" is *Elohim.* Here's the point: in verse 1, *Elohim* is translated as "God" (singular), and in verse 3, the

---

*\**Elohim* is a generic term for God that has come to be used as a name as well. Originally, *Elohim* meant "divine Being(s)," in contrast, for instance, to human being(s).

†Jewish scholars said that to avoid breaking the third commandment, "Thou shalt not take the name of the Lᴏʀᴅ thy God in vain" (Exodus 20:7), people shouldn't speak the holy name *YHWH.* Instead, they were to say *Adonai* (Lord). The name *Jehovah* used in the King James Version is composed of the consonants from *YHWH,* or *JHVH,* and the vowels (or an approximation thereof) from *Adonai.*

‡The word *Elohenu* that is used in Deuteronomy 6:4 is made up of *Elohim* and the suffix *nu,* "our." *Elohenu,* then, means "our God."

same Hebrew word is translated as "gods" (plural).

What justification is there for the translation of this word as a singular when the form is plural? Well, interestingly, while *Elohim* is plural, the verbs that are used with it are singular, and so are the pronouns the writers of the Bible used to refer to God. Genesis 1:27, for instance, says, "So God [*Elohim*, plural] *created* [singular] man in *his* [singular] own image, in the image of God [*Elohim*, plural] *created he* [both singular] him; male and female *created he* [both singular] them" (emphasis added).

This verse is not the only case where both singular and plural are used in reference to God. Genesis 3:22, Genesis 11, and other Old Testament passages follow this pattern too. Let's take a look at Genesis 11.

> And the Lord [*YHWH*, singular] said, Behold, the people is one, and they have all one language; and this they begin to do: and now nothing will be restrained from them, which they have imagined to do. Go to, let *us* [plural] go down, and there confound their language, that they may not understand one another's speech. So the Lord [singular] scattered them abroad from thence upon the face of all the earth: and they left off to build the city (verses 6–8; emphasis added).

Notice that in verses 6 and 8, the writer, Moses, speaks of God in the singular: He is the "Lord." Yet the Lord refers to Himself in the plural: "Let *us* . . ."

Isaiah followed the same pattern. He wrote,

And one [seraph] cried unto another, and said, *Holy, holy, holy,* is the LORD of hosts: the whole earth is full of *his* glory. . . .

Then said I, Woe is me! for I am undone; because I am a man of unclean lips, and I dwell in the midst of a people of unclean lips: for mine eyes have seen the *King,* the LORD of hosts. . . . I heard the voice of the *Lord,* saying, Whom shall I send, and who will go for *us*? Then said I, Here am I; send me (Isaiah 6:3, 5, 8; emphasis added).

This is one of the most important manifestations of God in the entire Bible. It contains the threefold "holy," which is probably related to the Three Divine Names in the *Sh'ma.* And while the writer refers to God in the singular ("the King," "the LORD of hosts," "his," "the Lord"), God refers to Himself in the plural ("who will go for *us*?").

Reducing complex expressions to simple forms can produce overly simplistic results, but sometimes, it highlights important truths instead; for example, Jesus summarized the Ten Commandments in the golden rule (Luke 10:27). So perhaps we can summarize what we've seen in the passages above as constituting a pattern that is significant to our understanding of the nature of God.

- When the sacred writer speaks about God, he uses the singular.
- When God speaks about Himself, He uses the plural.
- When the sacred author resumes the narrative, he again refers to God in the singular.

So, it is clear that the Hebrew Scriptures associate plurality and God.

Even the Zohar, which is foundational to Jewish mysticism, recognized that Jewish thinking includes the idea of plurality in unity. The passage from the Zohar that comments on the *Sh'ma* reads as follows:

> "Hear, O Israel, YHVH *Elohenu* YHVH is one."
> These three are one. How can the three Names be
> one? Only through the perception of Faith: in the
> vision of the Holy Spirit, in the beholding of the
> hidden eyes alone. The mystery of the audible voice
> is similar to this, for though it is one yet it consists
> of three elements—fire, air, and water, which have,
> however, become one in the mystery of the voice.
> Even so it is with the mystery of the threefold Di-
> vine manifestation designated by *YHVH Elohenu
> YHVH*—three modes which yet form one unity.[2]

The fact that *Elohim* is plural doesn't necessarily prove a tri-unity (the Trinity), but it does point in that direction. When viewed in light of the other evidences, its significance becomes even more impressive.

## The use of *Echad*

Deuteronomy 6:4 uses the word *echad* to express the unity, the Oneness, of God: "the LORD is one [*echad*]" (NKJV). Let's take a look at how this word is used in other parts of the Old Testament.

"And God called the light Day, and the darkness he called Night. And the evening and the morning were the first [*echad*] day" (Genesis 1:5). The New American Standard Bible (NASB) renders the same verse, "God called the light day, and the darkness He called night. And there was evening and there was morning, one [*echad*] day." Here we see two different manifestations of the day—darkness and light—that joined together compose one common unity called *day*.

*Echad* is also used in the case of marriage: "Therefore shall a man leave his father and his mother, and shall cleave unto his wife: and they shall be one [*echad*] flesh" (Genesis 2:24). Here the word *echad* indicates that when married, two different manifestations of humankind, a man and a woman, are "one" (*echad*) flesh. Each is an individual; each differs from the other; but they are compatible. When joined in marriage, they come into a unity so intimate that Scripture says they are one flesh.

Ezra 2:64 also uses the word *echad:* "The whole congregation together [*echad*] was forty and two thousand three hundred and threescore." Notice that the whole assembly is *echad.* This means that a group of thousands of people from diverse tribes and of all ages, educational levels, and occupations may be "one." So the word *echad* carries stronger connotations of unity than it does merely of the numeric figure "one."[3]

Ezekiel 37:17 provides another remarkable example. Here God tells the prophet to take two sticks "and join them one to another into one [*echad*] stick; and they shall become one in thine hand." Here two different sticks are held together and transformed into one stick.

It is clear from the examples we've seen that *echad* signifies a unity that encompasses diverse elements, and it implies that when these correspond, they become—even with their individual distinctions—a unified body. Ernest Klein observes that *echad* may mean "to be one," "to make one," "to unite," or "be united," "joined," "combined," "to become united," "unified," depending on the grammatical structure in which it is used.[4] In its richness, the Hebrew language provides a word for what we might call absolute or exclusive unity, a word that always means *one,* exclusively and without diverse interior components. The word is *yachid.*[5] This is *not* the word that is used in the *Sh'ma.*

How is it that these Three Members of the Godhead constitute *One unity*? They are united in nature, in purpose, in cooperation, and in planning. Though distinct Persons, They act as One. The fact that diversity within unity is implied in the use of *echad* has led some scholars to argue that the doctrine of the Trinity is foreshadowed in Deuteronomy 6:4.[6]

In summary, the *Sh'ma* provides evidence for plurality in the Godhead. This biblical statement contains a threefold usage of the names of the Lord; one of the names it contains is *Elohim,* which is a plural word; and the Hebrew word it uses to speak of God's unity is *echad,* which implies distinct but correlating elements and diversities at the heart of this unity.

## Other plurals of divinity

Genesis portrays God as saying, "*Let Us* make man in *Our image,* according to *Our likeness*" (Genesis 1:26, NKJV; emphasis added). The use of the plural pronouns without distinguishing among those who are spoken of indicates that this is a conversation among equals. (Notice also that the plurality God uses when speaking about Himself appears in triplicate here too.) The next verse says, "God created man in His own image; in the image of God He created him; male and female He created them" (NKJV).

Notice that verse 26 refers to God once again in that triple pattern of plurality and that in the very next verse there is a shift to the singular form. This use of the plural in Genesis 1:26 and elsewhere in the Old Testament has not slipped past theologians unobserved. Bible commentators, translators of the Hebrew Scriptures, and professors of theology have given much thought to it. The First Council of Sirmium, which met around the middle of the fourth century A.D., for instance, affirmed that Genesis 1:26 "was addressed by the Father to the Son as a distinct Person and threatened excommunication" to all Christians who denied this conclusion.[7]

In an article titled "The Meaning of 'Let Us' in Gn 1:26," Gerhard F. Hasel, seminary professor at Andrews University, discussed several options: (1) the mythological interpretation, (2) address to earthly elements, (3) address to the heavenly court, (4) the plural of majesty, (5) the plural of deliberation, and finally (6) the plural of fullness. He wrote,

> This plural [the "us" in Genesis 1:26] supposes that there is within the divine Being the distinction of personalities, a plurality within the deity, a "unanimity of intention and plan." In other words, a distinction in the divine Being with regard to a plurality of persons is here represented as a germinal idea. Thus the phrase "let us" expresses through its plural of fullness an intra-divine deliberation among "persons" within the divine Being. The understanding of

the plural as a plural of fullness gives all indications of being an adequate interpretation which avoids the unsatisfactory aspects of the other solutions. . . .

. . . If one considers such passages as Gn 3:22 and 11:7, and especially Dan 7:9-10, 13-14, along with Pr 8, it does not seem to be inconceivable that the writer of Gn 1 wished to imply in vs. 26 that in the creation of man a deliberating counseling between "persons" and a mutual summons within the deity or divine Being took place.[8]

In the rest of this chapter, we will look at several Old Testament passages in which more than One Divine Person is evident.

## At least Two Divine Persons

*Genesis 19:24.* In the biblical story of Sodom and Gomorrah, we find another kind of Old Testament hint at the plurality of the Godhead. The latter part of Genesis 18 (see, for example, verse 22) pictures Abraham bargaining with the "Lord" for the preservation of Sodom and Gomorrah. Then the next chapter says, "The *Lord* rained upon Sodom and upon Gomorrah brimstone and fire *from the Lord out of heaven*" (Genesis 19:24; emphasis added).

The passage seems to be saying that the Lord who came to examine Sodom and Gomorrah, who stayed to bargain with Abraham (Genesis 18:20–22), and who then rained brimstone and fire is a different Lord than the One in heaven from whom the brimstone and fire rained down on those two evil cities.

*Psalm 45:6, 7.* "Thy throne, O God [*Elohim*], is for ever

and ever: the sceptre of thy kingdom is a right sceptre. Thou lovest righteousness, and hatest wickedness: therefore God [*Elohim*], thy God [*Eloha*], hath anointed thee with the oil of gladness above thy fellows."

What captures the attention of teachers of Scripture in these two verses is that the psalmist's lyric says that because of the righteous orientation of One Person whom the psalmist calls God (the first *Elohim*), that Person has been anointed by His God (*Elohe*—another form of *El/Elohim*)—a Second Person who is called God. This seems to be a clear evidence for the plurality of the Godhead.

*Hosea 1:7.* "I will have mercy upon the house of Judah, and will save them by the Lord their God" (Hosea 1:7).

God is speaking, and He says that He will save them "by the Lord their God"—a case, again, of Two Persons called God.

*Zechariah 2:8, 9.* "For thus saith the Lord of hosts; After the glory hath he sent me unto the nations which spoiled you: for he that toucheth you toucheth the apple of his eye. For, behold, I will shake mine hand upon them, and they shall be a spoil to their servants: and ye shall know that the Lord of hosts hath sent me."

This is another case in which we observe the Lord being sent by another Lord.

## Three Divine Persons

*Isaiah 48:12–16.* "Hearken unto me, O Jacob and Israel, my called; *I am he; I am the first, I also am the last.* Mine hand also hath laid the foundation of the earth, and my right hand hath spanned the heavens: when I call unto them, they stand up together. All ye, assemble yourselves, and hear; which among them hath declared these things?

The LORD [*YHVH*] hath loved him: he will do his pleasure on Babylon, and his arm shall be on the Chaldeans. I, even I, have spoken; yea, I have called him: I have brought him, and he shall make his way prosperous.

"Come ye near unto me, hear ye this; I have not spoken in secret from the beginning; from the time that it was, there am I: and now the *Lord* GOD [*Adonai YHVH*], and his *Spirit* [*Ruach*], hath sent me" (emphasis added).

God, the Speaker and Revealer—"I am he"; the First Divine Person in the section—is presenting Himself as the "first and the last" (Revelation 2:8; John applies this to the Lord Jesus). At the end of the passage, the One who is speaking says that the "Lord GOD" (a Second Divine Person) and His "Spirit" (a Third Divine Person) are sending Him out to accomplish the task spoken of in this passage. It is evident that the concept of God that we find in the New Testament is anticipated in this Old Testament passage.

*Isaiah 63:7–14.* "I will mention the lovingkindnesses of the LORD, and the praises of the LORD, according to all that the LORD hath bestowed on us, and the great goodness toward the house of Israel, which he hath bestowed on them according to his mercies, and according to the multitude of his lovingkindnesses. For he said, Surely they are my people, children that will not lie: so *he was their Saviour.* In all their affliction he was afflicted, and *the angel of his presence* saved them: in his love and in his pity he redeemed them; and he bare them, and carried them all the days of old.

"But they rebelled, and vexed *his holy Spirit:* therefore he was turned to be their enemy, and he fought against them. Then he remembered the days of old, Moses, and his people, saying, Where is he that brought them up out of the sea with the shepherd of his flock? where is he that put *his holy Spirit* within him? That led them by the right hand of Moses with his glorious arm, dividing the water before them, to make himself an everlasting name? That led them through the deep, as an horse in the wilderness, that they should not stumble? As a beast goeth down into the valley, *the Spirit of the Lord* caused him to rest: so didst thou lead thy people, to make thyself a glorious name" (emphasis added).

In this passage, the Lord (*YHWH*) is referred to in verse 7. He then appears as the Angel of the His—the Lord's—Presence (verse 9), as the Holy Spirit (*Ruach ha kadosh,* verses 10 and 11), and as the Spirit of the Lord (*Ruach YHWH,* verse 14).

There is One God who made the exodus of Israel from Egypt possible; but here Isaiah writes of Three Divine Beings, and I believe that nothing refutes the idea that all Three belong within the unity of the Godhead.

## Summary

Without a doubt, in the Old Testament, the concept of God is associated with plurality. We have seen plurality implied in the choice of terms used to describe the personhood of God. We've found that when God spoke of Himself, He at times used plural pronouns. This use of the plural suggests that there are distinct personalities within the Divine Being. This concept of plurality in the Godhead is taken up in the Psalms and by various prophets, including Hosea, Zechariah, and Isaiah.

This abundant evidence leads us to conclude that the idea that the Old Testament offers evidence of the tri-unity of God has not been contrived by reading this view into the text. On the contrary, it flows *from* the text of the Old Testament, indicating that God deliberately intended to reveal His plurality to those who would read the Scriptures with care.

There is one God, and that God is threefold—holy, holy, holy!

1. Some of the elements in this chapter are taken from my book *Credos Contemporáneos* [*Contemporary Beliefs*] (Buenos Aires: Asociación Casa Editora Sudamericana, 1995).

2. Moses ben Maimón, "The Thirteen Principles of Faith," in *Zohar* 3 (London: Soncino Press, 1949), 134; quoted in Samuel Srolovic Jacobson, *The Quest of a Jew* (Washington, D.C.: Review and Herald® Publishing Association, 1973), 11. This is also referred to as *Zohar Shemot* 43b. See also "Don't Christians Believe in Three Gods?" Jews for Jesus, http://jewsforjesus.org/answers/theology/believeinthreegods.

3. Wilhelm Gesenius, *Gesenius's Hebrew and Chaldee Lexicon to the Old Testament Scriptures,* trans. Samuel Prideaux Tregelles (New York: John Wiley & Sons, 1965), 28.

4. Ernest Klein, *A Comprehensive Etymological Dictionary of the Hebrew Language for Readers of English* (New York: MacMillan Publishing, 1987), 17.

5. Jacobson, *The Quest of a Jew,* 12. See also R. Laird Harris, Gleason L. Archer, and Bruce K. Waltke, *Theological Wordbook of the Old Testament,* ed. R. Laird Harris (Chicago: Moody Press, 1980), s.v. "echad."

6. See Harris, Archer, and Waltke, *Theological Wordbook,* s.v. "echad."

7. H. H. Somers, "The Riddle of a Plural (Gen 1: 26): Its History in Tradition," *Folia Studies in the Christian Perpetuation of the Classics* 9 (1955): 63–67; quoted in Gerhard F. Hasel, "The Meaning of 'Let Us' in Gn 1:16," *Andrews University Seminary Studies* 13, no. 1 (Spring 1975): 59.

8. Hasel, "The Meaning of 'Let Us' in Gn 1:16," 65, 66.

# Chapter 3

# Tri-unity in the New Testament

The New Testament reveals God more clearly and directly than does the Hebrew Scriptures. As the Revealer of His Father, Christ becomes the link between God and humankind in all aspects of the believers' daily lives. God, now manifested in the flesh, is the object of prayer, praise, and worship. What He reveals in the New Testament Scriptures, more clearly than ever before, becomes the object of careful searching, meditation, prayer, and transmission among the community of faith.

In our brief review of pertinent Old Testament passages about God, we saw that they consistently describe Him as One God. However, even in the *Sh'ma,* which explicitly states the oneness of the Lord, we saw striking indications of plurality. We also noted that, starting early in Genesis and continuing on in the Old Testament, while the Bible writers speak of God in the singular, God frequently refers to Himself in the plural. Now we will look at the New Testament's much more direct and unambiguous revelation of the Godhead.

Matthew records Jesus as saying, "Go therefore and make disciples of all the nations, baptizing them in the name of the Father and of the Son and of the Holy Spirit" (Matthew 28:19, NKJV). Perhaps framing these words schematically makes the point stand out more clearly.

| The Name | | |
|:---:|:---:|:---:|
| Father | Son | Holy Spirit |

A candid reading of what Jesus said about baptism makes evident a simple fact: Jesus told the disciples to baptize all new Christians in the name (singular) of the Father, the Son, and the Holy Spirit (Three Persons; a plurality). The similarity of this formulation to what we saw in the Old Testament grabs our attention; in both, statements about God have elements of the singular and of the plural.

## The Godhead in the writings of Paul

In the conclusion to the Second Epistle to the Corinthians, the apostle Paul says, "The grace of the Lord Jesus Christ, and the love of God, and the communion of the Holy Spirit be with you all. Amen" (2 Corinthians 13:14, NKJV). Like Jesus, the apostle Paul, who was trained in the rabbinical schools that produced Gamaliel and Hillel and who had been a Pharisee, also names Three Divine Persons: Jesus, God, and the Holy Spirit.

Was Paul confused? Was he implying that there are Three Gods? The answer is found in the context: "Finally, brethren, farewell. Become complete. Be of good comfort, be of one mind, live in peace; and *the God* [in the Greek in which Paul wrote, this word is in the singular] of love and peace will be with you" (verse 11, NKJV; emphasis added). The context indicates that Paul is talking about One God.

Paul also employed the triple name—the Spirit, the Lord Jesus, and God—in his First Epistle to the Corinthians: "And such were some of you. But you were washed, but you were sanctified, but you were justified in the name of the *Lord Jesus* and by *the Spirit* of *our God*" (1 Corinthians 6:11, NKJV; emphasis added).

There can be no doubt that when the apostle Paul reflects

on the nature of God, he presents Him as a Godhead constituted of God, the Spirit, and the Lord Jesus. He pictures the Members of the Godhead in heaven as being characterized by closeness and unity, and says God means this to be replicated here on earth in the church. For the apostle, worship of God and service in His name require unity within the church even as its members exercise a diversity of callings. "There are diversities of gifts, but the same Spirit. There are differences of ministries, but the same Lord. And there are diversities of activities, but it is the same God who works all in all" (1 Corinthians 12:4–6, NKJV).

So here's the point, and it's an important one: the unity in diversity of the Godhead models for us how God intends the community of the elect, the church, to function. Without that model, the call to unity in diversity that Paul made for his day and for ours wouldn't be nearly as clear and as strong.

When we are in tune with this Pauline perception of God, we can see its consistency with the Old Testament concept, and we can begin to comprehend the roles and functions within the Godhead.

The following passages enlarge our picture of Paul's perception of God.

> He who sows to his flesh will of the flesh reap corruption, but he who sows to the Spirit will of the Spirit reap everlasting life. And let us not grow weary while doing good, for in due season we shall reap if we do not lose heart. Therefore, as we have opportunity, let us do good to all, especially to those who are of the household of faith. See with what large letters

I have written to you with my own hand! As many as desire to make a good showing in the flesh, these would compel you to be circumcised, only that they may not suffer persecution for the cross of Christ. For not even those who are circumcised keep the law, but they desire to have you circumcised that they may boast in your flesh. But God forbid that I should boast except in the cross of our Lord Jesus Christ, by whom the world has been crucified to me, and I to the world. For in Christ Jesus neither circumcision nor uncircumcision avails anything, but a new creation (Galatians 6:8–15, NKJV).

Now He who establishes us with you in Christ and has anointed us is God, who also has sealed us and given us the Spirit in our hearts as a guarantee (2 Corinthians 1:21, 22, NKJV).

God's tri-unity receives renewed emphasis in Paul's apostolic farewell. God's faithful servant draws from the unity of the Godhead a powerful model of conduct and purpose for all those who share in the divine commission on earth: "Rejoice always, pray without ceasing, in everything give thanks; for this is the will of God in Christ Jesus for you. Do not quench the Spirit. Do not despise prophecies. Test all things; hold fast what is good. Abstain from every form of evil" (1 Thessalonians 5:16–22, NKJV).

## The Godhead in the writings of Peter

We find in the writings of Peter consistency with the picture of the Godhead we saw in the Old Testament and elsewhere in the New Testament. Peter was a member of the inner circle among Jesus' disciples. Peter was born a Jew; his familiarity with the Scriptures grew in depth under the Master's guidance; and his two epistles are important parts of the New Testament.

The introduction to his first epistle says, "Peter, an apostle of Jesus Christ, to the pilgrims of the Dispersion in Pontus, Galatia, Cappadocia, Asia, and Bithynia, elect according to the foreknowledge of God the Father, in sanctification of the Spirit, for obedience and sprinkling of the blood of Jesus Christ: Grace to you and peace be multiplied" (1 Peter 1:1, 2, NKJV). This introduction shows that Peter believed in the One God of his fathers, whose plurality is now seen to be personified in the Father, the Spirit, and Jesus Christ. In his testimony, Peter reveals that his fellow apostles and the Christian church they serve are in tune with this unfolding understanding of the Godhead.

## Summary

We have seen that the New Testament's picture of God is in harmony with that of the Old Testament. Jesus instructed His followers to baptize in "the name" of God, but He clarified that that name includes the Three Divine Persons of the Godhead. Paul portrays the One God to be composed of the Father, the Son, and the Holy Spirit, and he expounds on the unity of the church despite its diversity of gifts as modeled on the unity of the Three Members of the Godhead despite Their differing responsibilities. Peter presents the same view of God, one that stands in harmony with the Old Testament Scriptures and with the epistles of his fellow apostles. The writings of these servants of God— men who have different backgrounds yet who belong to the same community of faith—are all in agreement.

## Chapter 4

# Matthew Calls Jesus "God"

In chapter 40 of the book of Isaiah, there is a reference
that over the centuries has captured the attention of many
Bible students. The Jewish community has identified this
chapter as a "comforting" portion of Scripture because it
begins with the loving words "Comfort ye, comfort ye my
people" and goes on to say, "Speak tenderly to Jerusalem"
(verse 2, NRSV).

Verse 3 of this chapter calls on God's people to "prepare . . . the way of the LORD." You most likely have noticed
that in your English translation the word LORD is written
with capital letters (large and small capitals). As we noted
earlier in this book, when this word is capitalized in this
way, it indicates that the original text contains the sacred
name of God—*YHWH* or *JHVH*—a name the Jews considered to be so sacred that they wouldn't even speak it lest
they be guilty of taking God's name in vain. The writers of
Scripture never used this name for any other divinity or god.
So, we see in this passage that Isaiah the prophet was invit-
ing the Hebrew people to prepare the way for the coming of
the Lord, the God of Israel.

The New International Version translates verse 3 this
way: "A voice of one calling: 'In the desert prepare the way
for the Lord; make straight in the wilderness a highway for
our God.' " In footnotes, it offers these alternative translations: *"A voice of one calling in the desert: / 'Prepare the way
for the Lord' "* and *"make straight a highway for our God."*

Undoubtedly, the apostle Matthew considered the ministry

of the Lord Jesus to be the fulfillment of this prophecy. In fact, he says so straight out: "For this is he who was spoken of by the prophet Isaiah, saying: 'The voice of one crying in the wilderness: "Prepare the way of the LORD; make His paths straight" ' " (Matthew 3:3, NKJV). The author of the fourth Gospel applies the prophetic anticipation of the coming of the Lord to the Lord Jesus. Set out schematically, the point is clear.

| Old Testament | New Testament |
|---|---|
| "The voice of him that crieth in the wilderness, Prepare ye the way of the LORD [*YHWH*], make straight in the desert a highway for our God" (Isaiah 40:3). | "This [John the Baptist, see verses 1, 2] is he that was spoken of by the prophet Esaias [Isaiah], saying, The voice of one crying in the wilderness, Prepare ye the way of the Lord [*Kurios*], make his paths straight" (Matthew 3:3). |

Breaking these texts down to their bare bones, we have the following.

| Old Testament | New Testament |
|---|---|
| LORD (God) | Lord (Jesus) |
| *YHWH* | *Kurios* |

In other words, the New Testament clearly and directly applies the holy name of the God of Hebrew Scripture to the Lord Jesus Christ.

## God with us

Another incident in which Matthew drew from the book of Isaiah has attracted the attention of numerous scholars.

I'll put it directly in a chart.

| Old Testament | New Testament |
|---|---|
| "Therefore the Lord himself shall give you a sign; Behold, a virgin shall conceive, and bear a son, and shall call his name Immanuel" (Isaiah 7:14). | "Now all this was done, that it might be fulfilled which was spoken of the Lord by the prophet, saying, Behold, a virgin shall be with child, and shall bring forth a son, and they shall call his name Emmanuel, which being interpreted is, God with us" (Matthew 1:22, 23). |
| Immanuel = "God with us" | Jesus is the fulfillment of this prophecy, so He is "God with us." |

Matthew says the Lord Jesus was the fulfillment of the prophesied miraculous conception and birth in Bethlehem, and he applies the name *Emmanuel,* "God with us," directly to Jesus.

Jesus, then, is "God with us."

In other words, *Jesus is God!*

# A Messianic Psalm

The book of Psalms was the hymnbook of the people of Israel. Just as we use our hymnbooks as sources of songs to sing in honor of the Lord, so the Jewish people found in Psalms songs to sing in the temple at their yearly festivals, and every Sabbath in their homes and their synagogues. Like our songs today, the psalms conveyed the message of God's Word, calling the people of the Lord to walk in His laws every day of their lives.

One day the Sadducees and Pharisees questioned Jesus, hoping to trip Him up. He answered their questions—satisfactorily, of course—and then queried them in turn. "What do you think of the Messiah?" He asked. "Whose Son is He?" (See Matthew 22:42.)

Jesus' opponents answered that the Messiah was to be a Son of David. Their answer set Jesus up to toss a tough but crucial question to them: "How then doth David . . . call him Lord, saying, The LORD said unto my Lord, Sit thou on my right hand, till I make thine enemies thy footstool? If David then call him Lord, how is he his son?" (verses 43–45).

The Bible says nobody could answer Jesus' question. No doubt there was a deep silence. But silence doesn't mean absence of thinking. I don't imagine the Sadducees and Pharisees were the only people who heard Jesus' question. I think the disciples did, too, and I'm sure they continued to puzzle over it. What *was* the meaning of that line in Psalm 110: "The LORD said unto my Lord . . ."?

The book of Acts tells us the conclusion reached by those who had heard Jesus ask that question and who now were His apostles and witnesses. In the sermon Peter preached on the Day of Pentecost, he quoted that line from Psalm 110 again, but now he added a groundbreaking answer—an answer revealed by the light of the ministry of Jesus, His crucifixion, His resurrection, and His ascension into heaven, which had absolutely transformed the early church. Peter said, "For David is not ascended into the heavens: but he saith himself, The LORD said unto my Lord, Sit thou on my right hand, until I make thy foes thy footstool. Therefore let all the house of Israel know assuredly, that God hath made that same Jesus, whom ye have crucified, both *Lord* and *Christ*" (Acts 2:34–36; emphasis added).

# Chapter 5

# Jesus as God in the Gospel of John

John's Gospel is a testimony written by a Jew who was familiar with the Messianic expectations of his fellow Jews (John 1:21; 4:25; 6:14; 7:40–42). The beloved apostle provided the testimony of people who had known Jesus firsthand—people who were drawing from well-remembered experiences, who were known personally by the apostle, and who had valuable perspectives to share. Masterfully, John gathered the testimonies of these witnesses and used them and his own recollections to compose this final Gospel. Notice some of the witnesses whose perspectives he brought into the telling:

- John the Baptist, who proclaimed, "Behold the Lamb of God, which taketh away the sin of the world" (John 1:29).
- Andrew, brother of Peter, who stated, "We have found the Messias" (verse 41).
- Nathanael, who exclaimed, "Rabbi, thou art the Son of God; thou art the King of Israel" (verse 49).
- Nicodemus, who, at midnight, confessed, "Rabbi, we know that thou art a teacher come from God: for no man can do these miracles that thou doest, except God be with him" (John 3:2).
- The Samaritan woman at Jacob's well, who unabashedly announced, "Come, see a man, which told me all things that ever I did: is not this the Christ?" (John 4:29).
- The chief priests and Pharisees in council, who

nervously wondered aloud after Jesus resurrected Lazarus, "What do we? for this man doeth many miracles" (John 11:47).

* And Thomas, who, in undoubting reverence, finally uttered, "My Lord and my God" (John 20:28).

John himself was a witness. More than five thousand were miraculously fed on a grassy knoll, and John was present. Lazarus was called back to life, and John saw it with his own eyes. Thomas, a disciple who had lost his faith, returned to belief when he saw the resurrected Jesus, and John was there too. Thomas's deeply emotional words "My Lord and my God" (John 20:28) would never fade from John's mind.

The Gospel of John has special worth for Christian readers; it is the testimony of the last living disciple of Christ. John chose his words with thoughtful care because he wanted us to know how much Jesus meant to him. It is of great significance that this apostle, raised in the hope offered in the Hebrew Scriptures, realized that his Lord Jesus truly is the Living God.

John wanted to make sure we clearly understand this truth. With his opening remarks, he launched right into the heart of his testimony, immediately directing the reader's focus to the person of Jesus and His divine relationship with God. "In the beginning was the Word, and the Word was with God, and the Word was God. The same was in the beginning with God. All things were made by him; and without him was not any thing made that was made" (John 1:1–3).

The context makes it clear that the Word John was speaking about is a Person (verse 12), and that Person is God. It would be a mistake to translate this passage as "the Word was [a] God." That unwarranted interpretation made by one esteemed religious community unfortunately misses John's meaning, which is the testimonial objective laid out in this chapter and supported throughout the Gospel.*

Verse 3 says, "Without him was not any thing made that was made." This text reinforces the idea that the Word is God. The Word is *cause,* not *consequence.* The Word produces or carries out creation, but the Word Himself is by no means the product of any other creative force. Because He is the *Logos,* He is therefore the Creator. From eternity He was with God, and He is God. Through Him all that exists came into existence.

Having made that profound assertion about the Word's role in creation, John now moves to the next level, disclosing just exactly who the Word really is. To follow this logic we must bear in mind that Jewish writers naturally used Hebrew imagery. We must remember that God spoke from the sanctuary; it was there that Moses and Aaron found guidance and heard His voice. There, in the Most Holy Place, the *Shekinah* beamed its glory.

John sent a strong, clear message to any among his readers who might have been confused about what he just declared. He told us exactly what he meant. "And the Word was made flesh, and dwelt among us, (and we beheld his glory, the glory as of the only begotten of the Father,) full of grace and truth" (John 1:14).

John's message is clear and decisive: The Word that he was speaking about is a Person. More than that, though, the Word became flesh, He is God.

---

*The vast majority of Bible translations render the meaning of the text just as does the King James Version: "the Word was God."

John explains by telling us that Christ "dwelt among us." The Greek verb translated as "dwelt" is *eskēnōsen,* which is derived from the word *skēnē,* meaning "tent." The word *skēnē* was used in the Septuagint, the Greek version of the Old Testament, to refer to the "tent of the meeting"—the tabernacle, in other words. In several texts in the New Testament, *skēnē* is used to indicate the place where God lives (see, for example, Hebrews 8:2; Revelation 13:6). John has a parallel in mind: the Old Testament portrays God as living among His people in the tent, the *skēnē,* of meeting, and now Jesus has come to "tent" (*skenoō*) among His people— to dwell among them. And "we beheld his glory," exclaims John. From the prophet Isaiah through Matthew and now John comes the message of "Immanuel"—"God with us" (Isaiah 7:14; 8:8; Matthew 1:23).

## A surprising translation

John is enraptured with the preexistent Jesus: "No one has ever seen God, but the one and only Son, who is himself God and is in closest relationship with the Father, has made him known" (John 1:18, NIV, 2011). The 2011 New International Version expresses it well when it says that Jesus is the "only Son, who is himself God." Other modern versions render that weighty verse as follows:

- "No one has ever seen God, but God the One and Only, who is at the Father's side, has made him known" (NIV, 1984).
- "No one has seen God at any time; the only begotten God who is in the bosom of the Father, He has explained Him" (NASB).

- "No one has ever seen God; the only God, who is at the Father's side, he has made him known" (ESV).
- "No one has ever seen God. But the unique One, who is himself God, is near to the Father's heart. He has revealed God to us" (NLT).
- "No one has ever seen God. The unique God, who is close to the Father's side, has revealed him" (ISV).

The renditions of modern versions differ somewhat from the King James Version, which says that Jesus is "the only begotten Son, which is in the bosom of the Father." The King James Version is based on the *Textus Receptus*.* However, the majority of modern scholars render the verse according to older manuscripts in which Jesus is called the *monogenēs theos*[1]—"the only God," "the only begotten God," or "the only one God."

The apostle John is telling the readers of his Gospel that he wants them to know Jesus as the One and only God, who is at the Father's side, whom he, John, personally knows. "Jesus is so intimate with God, that he is one with God and can reveal him to men. In Jesus Christ the distant, unknowable, invisible, unreachable God has come to men; and God can never be a stranger to us again."[2]

## The I AM

As we have noted, God has given us the Bible to serve primarily as His revelation about Himself. The eventful manifestations of God that it records—known as *theophanies*

---

*The *Textus Receptus* ("Received Text") is the collection of Greek texts that served as the basis for the translation of various New Testament versions, such as those that are in Luther's German Bible and the King James Version.

(from *theo,* "God," and *phainein,* "shown")—took place in a wide variety of settings and times: in the wilderness, on mountaintops, on stormy seas, in the darkness of midnight, and under the noontime sun.

The theophany that set the stage for all subsequent revelations of God took place in the remote Midian desert. The Godhead had protected the youthful Moses in Egypt, but this mysterious revelation was the first encounter in which Moses was brought directly before the Lord. In that historical moment of empowerment, the Lord told Moses that He had heard the cry of His people, and He would use Moses to deliver them. Moses responded by saying that he needed to know who was sending him to deliver Israel out of bondage. Who, he asked, was this Deity, by what name should he make Him known? "And God said unto Moses, I AM THAT I AM: and he said, Thus shalt thou say unto the children of Israel, I AM hath sent me unto you" (Exodus 3:14).

Elaborating on the meaning of the I AM, John I. Durham wrote,

> "I AM that I AM," replies God. The verbs . . . [connote] continuing, unfinished action: "I am that I am being," or "I am the Is-ing One," that is, "the One Who Always Is." Not conceptual being, being in the abstract, but active being, is the intent of this reply. It is a reply that suggests that it is inappropriate to refer to God as "was" or as "will be," for the reality of this active existence can be suggested only by the present: "is" or "is-ing," "Always Is," or "Am."[3]

That story became fixed in the memory of the people of

Israel. Since the days of Moses, the name *I AM* has identified the One true God of Israel.

In the fullness of time, Jesus claimed this emblematic
name as His own. Under inspiration, John recognized His
right to that name, and in his Gospel, he recorded many
instances of Jesus' use of that holiest of names.

- "And Jesus said unto them, *I am* the bread of life: he
  that cometh to me shall never hunger; and he that
  believeth on me shall never thirst" (John 6:35; see
  also 6:48, 51; 7:28, 29).*
- "The Jews then murmured at him, because he said,
  *I am* the bread which came down from heaven"
  (John 6:41).
- "Then spake Jesus again unto them, saying, *I am* the
  light of the world: he that followeth me shall not
  walk in darkness, but shall have the light of life"
  (John 8:12).
- "Jesus said unto them, Verily, verily, I say unto you,
  Before Abraham was, *I am*" (verse 58).
- "Then said Jesus unto them again, Verily, verily, I
  say unto you, *I am* the door of the sheep" (John
  10:7; see also verse 9).
- "*I am* the good shepherd: the good shepherd giveth
  his life for the sheep" (verse 11; see also verse 14).
- "Jesus said unto her, *I am* the resurrection, and the
  life: he that believeth in me, though he were dead,
  yet shall he live" (John 11:25).
- "Jesus saith unto him, *I am* the way, the truth, and

---

*The emphasis in this text, and in those that follow in this list, has
been added.

the life: no man cometh unto the Father, but by me" (John 14:6).

- "Believest thou not that *I am* in the Father, and the Father in me? the words that I speak unto you I speak not of myself: but the Father that dwelleth in me, he doeth the works" (verse 10; see also verses 11, 20).

- "*I am* the vine, ye are the branches: He that abideth in me, and I in him, the same bringeth forth much fruit: for without me ye can do nothing" (John 15:5; see also verse 1).

The meaning of "I AM" is very clear in the writings of John. The apostle doesn't hesitate to report the offense the Jewish religious leaders took at these assertions. He emphasizes each of them as if working in a code that he knew would be recognized by those familiar with the divine name that was at the heart of Israel's history. He considers, too, the freeing of Israel from Egyptian slavery to be a sample of the Savior's mission—His work of freeing humankind from slavery to sin. John also remembers that Jesus didn't hesitate to appropriate this name for Himself. The sublime lesson to be drawn from John's use of those phrases is that the beloved apostle is revealing *who Jesus really is.* In effect, he's saying, "Behold, this Jesus known personally to me and upon whose breast I rested my head *is the very God—the I AM*—who centuries ago spoke to Moses at the burning bush!"

Evidences of the divine origin of Jesus are repeatedly interjected into John's telling of the gospel story. Perhaps it is because of the purposeful subtlety of that embedding that the casual reader skims along without discerning John's marvelous code. To know that Jesus truly is God is purely a gift from the Spirit, which, if we are receptive, will open for us just as it did for John.

## His intimacy with the Father

In the Gospel of John there is further and especially treasured evidence that deserves our close attention in our study of this topic. I refer to the numerous references Jesus lets fall from His lips that reveal the degree of His intimacy with God the Father before His incarnation. Through John's book, the Spirit unveils Jesus' role as Lord *even before* His coming as the historical Son of man to set into fulfillment mode all that was prefigured in the ancient Hebrew Scriptures.

As we read John's Gospel, we are awed by insights that flash brilliantly like jewels set in the apostle's memory—living words he heard from the mouth of Jesus Himself, telling His listeners that *He was sent by the Father* (John 8:16, 18); that *He was not from this world* (verse 23); that *He is One with His Father* (John 10:30); that when He was with the Father, *He was glorious* (John 17:5); and that *those who have seen Him have seen the Father* (John 14:9).

When we consider such references as those just cited, we are struck by the realization that no other human being could ever truthfully make such claims about himself. This realization tells us yet again that it was the Holy Spirit who moved John to reveal that though the Lord Jesus was clothed in human flesh, He came down to earth from the Eternal Godhead.

## The tri-unity concept in John

John 14 begins with Christ's promise to the disciples and to His faithful followers of all time that He will return to gather them home with Him. It is a message that manifests His loving care for all those who accept Him as their Savior. Jesus gave this message when deeply discouraging events were about to befall His disciples. In a matter of hours, they would see their Master spit upon, scourged, and nailed to a cross. Before those cruel scenes unfolded, Jesus made the comforting promise that He would not leave them to walk alone; He would return. "Let not your heart be troubled: ye believe in God, believe also in me. In my Father's house are many mansions: if it were not so, I would have told you. I go to prepare a place for you. And if I go and prepare a place for you, I will come again, and receive you unto myself; that where I am, there ye may be also" (John 14:1–3).

We notice that the promise is followed by an important series of questions and answers that allow Jesus to plant important ideas that increased the disciples' understanding of what they would experience. I have simplified and condensed that interchange without changing the order.

Q: [Thomas] "Lord, we know not whither thou goest; and how can we know the way?" (verse 5).

A: [Jesus] "I am the way, the truth, and the life: no man cometh unto the Father, but by me. If ye had known me, ye should have known my Father also: and from henceforth ye know him, and have seen him" (verses 6, 7).

Q: [Philip] "Lord, shew us the Father, and it sufficeth us" (verse 8).

A: [Jesus] "Have I been so long time with you, and yet hast thou not known me, Philip? he that hath seen me hath seen the Father; and how sayest thou then, Shew us the Father?" (verse 9).

Without a doubt, this was the clearest disclosure yet to the disciples of the Son's divine nature. In the book of John, the evidence placing Jesus within the Godhead is unambiguous. Revealing as that is, we shall see that there is even more. In this same chapter, Jesus goes on to explain how God would continue to be present among them in Jesus' absence.

Just what was to become of the disciples and all of the other believers when Jesus returned to heaven? Would God fill the gap for those who had to carry on in His name after the Son of man had gone, and if so, how would He do it?

Anticipating those insecurities, Jesus promised His followers that He wouldn't leave them comfortless. As He set their minds at rest, Jesus opened before them a wonderful vision into the triune nature and ministry of God. He said, "I will pray the Father, and he shall give you another Comforter, that he may abide with you for ever; Even the Spirit of truth; whom the world cannot receive, because it seeth him not, neither knoweth him: but ye know him; for he dwelleth with you, and shall be in you. I will not leave you comfortless: I will come to you" (verses 16–18).

In promising the disciples that they would not be left alone, Jesus made some very significant points. He said that He would "pray [to] the Father" (verse 16). In other words, He was saying that He was not the Father. We can draw from this the fact that Jesus and the Father are Two different Persons.

At this point, then, a Third Person of the Godhead enters. It is clear that the promised Comforter is neither the Father nor the Son. Several Greek words express the idea of the "other." The word John used as he recalled what the Master said on that occasion is *allos*. "The Greek word *allos* distinguishes the subject who is speaking from someone else."[4] The otherness indicated by this Greek word specifies a distinct person but one who ranks as an equal. Note also that the unity between Jesus and the Comforter is so close that Jesus can say, "I will not leave. . . . I will come to you" (verse 18, NIV). The presence of the Comforter is essentially the same as the presence of Jesus.

Jesus was a real Person, so it makes little sense to argue that He could be replaced by an impersonal thing or force. Yet those who deny the personhood of the Holy Spirit are left with this conclusion. Such a depersonalized concept of the Comforter undercuts the promise of personal presence Jesus made to the disciples.

The diagram below succinctly demonstrates the traditional understanding of the tri-unity of God held by Christians over many centuries.

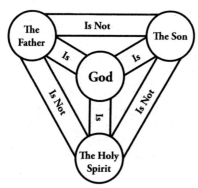

### At the end of the Gospel

As John concluded his Gospel, he reiterated the central message, drawing upon an experience that he couldn't forget. He chose to bring that incident into play to reinforce the basic premise of his entire Gospel.

Jesus, the disciples' beloved Master, had been crucified. They felt heartbroken, their hopes shattered. With their own eyes, they had seen His agony and then His dying the most horrible of all possible deaths. The pain penetrated so deeply into their hearts that it largely obscured all that Jesus had told them about what would happen to Him. Their minds were clouded with discouragement and numbing frustration; and a thick cloak of grief prevented them from sensing any hope.

So, when Thomas was told that the rest of the disciples had seen the risen Savior, he doubted the report. His spirit weakened by loss of faith, he stumbled into skepticism. John's narrative reveals this.

> But Thomas, one of the twelve, called Didymus, was not with them when Jesus came. The other disciples therefore said unto him, We have seen the Lord. But he said unto them, Except I shall see in his hands the print of the nails, and put my finger into the print of the nails, and thrust my hand into his side, I will not believe.
>
> And after eight days again his disciples were within, and Thomas with them: then came Jesus, the doors being shut, and stood in the midst, and said, Peace be unto you. Then saith he to Thomas, Reach hither thy finger, and behold my hands; and reach hither thy hand, and thrust it into my side: and be not faithless, but believing. And Thomas answered and said unto him, My Lord and my God (John 20:24–28).

John spells out the conditions Thomas had set for believing: "Except I shall see in his hands the print of the nails, and put my finger into the print of the nails, and thrust my hand into his side, I will not believe." Thomas refused to be hoodwinked into believing what might cause him further disillusionment. Only tangible evidence—viewing and touching—would work for him.

Jesus appeared again, this time when Thomas was present. He walked over to the doubter and invited him to touch the scars that he might at last believe. And then Thomas, overwhelmed by the evidence, acknowledged Jesus, calling Him, "My Lord and my God" (verse 28). Thomas was convinced that Jesus was truly the Lord of the *Sh'ma,* the very Lord and God spoken of in the Psalms.

John's awesome Gospel is the Spirit's gift to all Christians that we might also believe in Jesus as our Lord and Savior, the fullness of God revealed in human flesh.

1. Kurt Aland et al., eds., *The Greek New Testament,* 3rd ed. (New York: United Bible Societies, 1975), 322, reads *monogenes theos,* based on a majority of ancient sources.

2. William Barclay, *The Gospel of John,* rev. ed., The Daily Study Bible (Philadelphia: Westminster Press, 1975), 1:74, 75.

3. John I. Durham, *Exodus,* Word Biblical Commentary (Waco, Tex.: Word Books, 1987), 3:39.

4. Walter Bauer, *A Greek-English Lexicon of the New Testament and Other Early Christian Literature,* ed. Frederick William Danker, trans. William F. Arndt and F. Wilbur Gingrich (Chicago: University of Chicago Press, 2000), 46.

# Chapter 6
# Jesus in the Book of Revelation

The apostle John wrote three "sets" of books that are in the New Testament: his Gospel, three epistles, and the book of Revelation.[1] As previously mentioned, John was of a Hebrew mind. Regarding him, William Barclay, the well-known Bible commentator, wrote, "Greek is certainly not his native language; and it is often clear that he is writing in Greek and thinking in Hebrew."[2] John's writings reveal the influence of the Jewish culture, language, and faith in which he grew up. "He is steeped in the Old Testament. He quotes it or alludes to it 245 times. These quotations come from about twenty Old Testament books; his favourites are: Isaiah, Daniel, Ezekiel, Psalms, Exodus, Jeremiah, [and] Zechariah."[3]

John felt a deep responsibility to share his personal testimony and witness through his writings. In the Gospel account, John adds to his own recognition of Christ's divinity the words of other witnesses who knew the Master firsthand. Through each of these people, the Gospel of John proclaims Jesus' divinity.

The book of Revelation also extols the Divine Christ, but it has a different emphasis than does his Gospel—the ascended Jesus is no longer the Suffering Servant; He is Lord. In the introduction to Revelation, we see that though produced by John, the book literally depends on what Jesus Christ has decided to reveal; for as the title says, this is the revelation *of* Jesus Christ (Revelation 1:1). The book comprises two distinct sections: the first is historical, the second is eschatological. Clearly, however, the person of Jesus permeates the entire book—He is at the heart of both sections. And right from the start, John insists that this book is not an imaginatively created piece of fiction, like some popular novel dreamt up by a secular author. This is a message transmitted from Christ above, through His angel, to John, who testifies to everything he saw (verses 1, 2).

From the first chapter of this book and on, John gives us a series of captivating descriptions of what Jesus Christ is doing to draw the great controversy to a close. The scenes and words that flash into his mind, which he then scratches on parchment, stir the reader's wonder and call to mind prophetic utterances from the Old Testament. John reveals Jesus as "the faithful witness, the firstborn from the dead, and the ruler over the kings of the earth. . . . [The One] who loved us and washed us from our sins in His own blood" (verse 5, NKJV); the One who "cometh with clouds" (verse 7); "the Alpha and the Omega, . . . who is and who was and who is to come, the Almighty" (verse 8, NKJV; compare Revelation 22:13); "the Son of man" (Revelation 1:13); "the first and the last" (verse 17; compare Revelation 22:13); "he that liveth, and was dead; and . . . [is] alive for evermore, . . . and [has] the keys of hell and of death" (Revelation 1:18). All of this in just the first chapter! And through the rest of the twenty-two chapters, Revelation's portrayal of Jesus continues to grow like an algorithmic progression.

With celestial ease, these revelations come down to earth from boundless eternity and here begin to unfold the mysteries of Christ. They gather from Old Testament prophetic types, move along through scenes of His humiliation, and finally, lift all eyes up to the holy places of the heavenly sanctuary, portraying Jesus there not only as our High Priest but also as the Lord of lords who reigns forever.

John wants Revelation to, like his Gospel, reveal that Jesus, although human, is also much more than that, for He is equal to God. This fact becomes very clear as we examine the titles of Jesus that this book reveals.

Jesus is the Living Source and active protagonist of Revelation. This book's representation of Him goes far beyond that of the Gospels. Revelation shows us a Jesus permanently and gloriously transfigured. In this Apocalypse of John's, Jesus is enthroned and rules over the kings of the earth. Returned to the courts above, He doesn't work alone but rather in close relationship with His Father and the Spirit.

The humanity of Jesus is not lost or suppressed in Revelation. John tells us twice that Jesus is the Root of David. His book says Jesus was dead but now is alive. Though now the glorified humanity of Jesus transcends the borders of Judea and Canaan and He now dwells in glory, His humble earthly life does not vanish from memory. From infancy on, He was the constant target of Satan (Revelation 12:1–15), and the struggle rages on. But Jesus has ascended and is now interceding in order to end the great controversy in total victory.

In Revelation, there is a continuum between the Jesus who was humiliated and the Christ who stands next to the throne of God in the heavenly sanctuary. This scene is marvelously emphasized in Revelation. Although John doesn't directly call Jesus "God" in Revelation, he does present Him as equal to God.

## Evidence that Jesus is divine

Note in the following chart that Revelation applies terms to Jesus that are applied to God in the Old Testament.

| Applied to God in the Old Testament | Applied to Jesus in Revelation |
|---|---|
| "I am the Almighty God" (Genesis 17:1;* see also Genesis 28:3; 35:11; 43:14; 48:3; 49:25; Exodus 6:3; Numbers 24:4; etc.). | "The Almighty" (Revelation 1:8). |
| "For the LORD your God is God of gods, and Lord of lords, a great God, a mighty, and a terrible, which regardeth not persons, nor taketh reward" (Deuteronomy 10:17). | "These shall make war with the Lamb, and the Lamb shall overcome them: for he is Lord of lords, and King of kings: and they that are with him are called, and chosen, and faithful" (Revelation 17:14). |
| "I beheld till the thrones were cast down, and the Ancient of days did sit, whose garment was white as snow, and the hair of his head like the pure wool: his throne was like the fiery flame, and his wheels as burning fire" (Daniel 7:9). | "His head and his hairs were white like wool, as white as snow; and his eyes were as a flame of fire" (Revelation 1:14). |
| "Hearken unto me, O Jacob and Israel, my called; I am he; I am the first, I also am the last" (Isaiah 48:12). | "And when I saw him, I fell at his feet as dead. And he laid his right hand upon me, saying unto me, Fear not; I am the first and the last" (Revelation 1:17). |

*All the emphasis in this chart has been added.

Undoubtedly, the Jesus in Revelation differs from the Jesus in the Gospels. In Revelation, He is exalted and glorified. At the beginning of the book of Revelation, there is a trumpeting proclamation of the glorious Jesus, and thereafter, the figure and name of Jesus are given the highest honors through a series of titles, descriptions, and names, thus picturing for John's readers One who now is an awesome, exalted Being.

Jesus is He "that holdeth the seven stars in his right hand, who walketh in the midst of the seven golden candlesticks" (Revelation 2:1). This majestic representation pictures Him walking among His churches. In Revelation, Jesus is also called "the Lion of the tribe of Juda[h]" (Revelation 5:5). This was very meaningful to the Jewish people because it highlighted His connection to King David, the most valorous and beloved king of Israel. Through the centuries that followed the reign of David and Solomon, citizens of the kingdom of Judah maintained a wavering loyalty to God; consequently, the kingdom remained on the scene of history for centuries before apostasy eventually brought on the exile, though not the total destruction, of its people.

Up to this point all the titles mentioned in Revelation have connected Jesus with heaven. For example, He is a Victor who "also overcame, and . . . [was] set down with [his] Father in his throne" (Revelation 3:21), but as a human, He is also called "the Root of David" (Revelation 5:5). This is relevant in Jewish tradition; it indicates He came from the lineage of David. In Him, the author is telling us, the royal line on earth is connected with the royal line in heaven.

After John establishes this kingly connection, he compares our Savior to a lamb. In fact, Revelation applies the title *Lamb* to Jesus twenty-seven times. This title has two Christological functions. It says that Jesus is the Redeemer and that He is Lord in the sense of being a royal Ruler. In

Revelation, Jesus still bears the marks of His crucifixion (Revelation 5:6, 9, 10). The Lamb also connects Creation and Redemption, and it links the Exodus Passover with the liberation of fallen human beings from sin. It is only through the sacrifice of the Lamb that this greater Exodus has become possible.

So, Christ is the Lamb that stood "in the midst of the throne" (Revelation 5:6). He is the "Lamb slain from the foundation of the world" (Revelation 13:8), which John's Gospel says enabled Him to take away "the sin of the world" (John 1:29). From the beginning, God had planned this merciful ministry of the Savior to deal with the sin that marred our world. Because of His sacrifice, Christ can free and save all who will believe in Him (John 3:16).

As in the Gospel of John, here also Jesus is "Faithful and True" (Revelation 19:11). He is the "Word of God" (verse 13)—the *Logos* to those who spoke Greek, and the *memrah* for those who knew Hebrew. He is the "Word" that spoke from the tabernacle, the Word who had the power to create (John 1:3). He is the One who can make "all things new" (Revelation 21:5); the "bright and morning star" (Revelation 22:16); the One who "come[s] quickly" (verse 20).

Jesus' ministry in heaven maintains continuity with the ministry He had while on earth. Jesus' earthly ministry is evident in the figures employed in Revelation. While this Jesus, who now is exalted, was on earth, He was persecuted by the forces led by the dragon (Revelation 12:1–15). In Revelation, Jesus continues to be identified with the Jewish Messiah, who is called the "Son of man" (Revelation 1:13) and the "Root of David" (Revelation 5:5; 22:16), but He has gained greater stature because, after He was executed,

He came back to life (Revelation 1:18). In Revelation, it is clear that the Jesus who walked dusty Palestinian trails is the very One now exalted in heaven—the One who has existed from eternity (Revelation 3:14).

## What Revelation says about Christ

In his Gospel and his first epistle, John quite explicitly equates Jesus to God (John 1:1–3; 1 John 5:20). He doesn't do that in Revelation, but he does indirectly present Him as equal to God. As the chart shows, John applies to Christ some titles that the Old Testament applies to God. He also portrays Jesus as exercising divine privileges, qualities, and prerogatives. Jesus "searches . . . hearts" (Revelation 2:23, NKJV; cf. Jeremiah 17:10; Psalm 7:9). The priests who serve God serve Him as well (Revelation 20:6). He shares a throne with the Father (Revelation 22:1, 3). He is holy and true (Revelation 3:7; Isaiah 40:25). Significantly, Revelation, which specifically reserves worship for God (Revelation 19:10), pictures the entire universe worshiping Jesus along with God (Revelation 5:13).

In Revelation, Jesus manifests loving care for the church—the body of believers commissioned to carry the message of salvation through all history until the end of time and to all of the world. In this book, Jesus assures His faithful ones that He will be with them as they carry out their mission, and He promises to come again and take them to be with Him always.

1. A version of this chapter is available on the Internet. See Daniel Scarone, "Christ in the Book of Revelation," Adventist Pastor Online,

http://www.adventistpastoronline.com/index.php/christ-in-the-book-of-revelation/.

2. William Barclay, *The Revelation of John,* rev. ed., The Daily Study Bible (Philadelphia: Westminster Press, 1976), 1:12, 13.

3. Ibid., 12.

## Chapter 7
# Jesus in Other New Testament Writings

With marked consistency, New Testament writers affirm the divine nature of Jesus, of the Father, and of the Holy Spirit. They also confirm their unwavering belief in the teaching of the Old Testament that the Lord is One God. When, at times, detractors accused Christianity of polytheism, the apostles decidedly rejected those charges. This is borne out by the fact that when the New Testament speaks about the Father, the Son, and the Holy Spirit, it never uses the expression "Gods." There is only one reason for this: the God worshiped and adored by the disciples is One God.

### Jesus in Paul's epistles

The writings of the apostle Paul did much to nurture the thought of the early Christian church, presenting a more fully developed theology than did the other New Testament writers. Paul steadfastly upheld the divine nature of the Lord Jesus and the tri-unity of God, as the following material makes clear.

*The Epistle to the Romans.* In this epistle, Paul discloses his personal belief about who Jesus is. In referring to the Jewish lineage of Jesus, he says that He "is over all, God blessed for ever. Amen" (Romans 9:5). This text leaves no doubt about the fact that Jesus is God.

*The Epistle to the Philippians.* This letter contains one of the most important statements about Jesus. Let's look at it carefully.

Let this mind be in you, which was also in Christ
Jesus: who, being in the form of God, thought it not
robbery to be equal with God: but made himself of
no reputation, and took upon him the form of a
servant, and was made in the likeness of men: and
being found in fashion as a man, he humbled himself, and became obedient unto death, even the
death of the cross. Wherefore God also hath highly
exalted him, and given him a name which is above
every name: that at the name of Jesus every knee
should bow, of things in heaven, and things in earth,
and things under the earth; and that every tongue
should confess that Jesus Christ is Lord, to the glory
of God the Father (Philippians 2:5–11).

The New International Version renders verse 6 this
way: "Who, being in very nature God, did not consider
equality with God something to be grasped." Paul is speaking here explicitly about the nature of Jesus, and he unabashedly declares that Jesus is God. He goes on, then, to
promote the worship of Christ not only by human beings
but also by the entire universe. Paul knew that there are
legitimate boundaries between true and false worship, yet
he felt free to call us to render to Jesus the same honor we
offer to God.

*The Epistle to the Colossians.* In this letter, Paul touches
again upon the topic of the person of Jesus, adding one
more link to the growing chain of powerful statements on
this topic. "Beware," he writes, "lest any man spoil you
through philosophy and vain deceit, after the tradition of
men, after the rudiments of the world, and not after Christ.

For in him dwelleth all the fullness of the Godhead bodily" (Colossians 2:8, 9).

The apostle says that "all the fullness of the Godhead" dwells in Jesus. How could anyone be clearer or more direct?

Paul wrote this letter to counter a controversy involving false teaching—a kind of mysticism bordering on Gnosticism that was distorting the true focus of worship so that some Christians in Colossae were being tempted to worship angels. (See Colossians 2:18.) Paul counsels them to beware of such practices. They're intended to captivate minds. They lead people away from Christ. It is in this context of false worship—worship of the unworthy—that the apostle reminds believers that it is in Christ that "all the fullness of the Godhead [dwells] bodily." It is the purpose of this powerful apostolic statement to draw the Colossian believers back from a growing but misguided cult of angels to the rightful worship of the Lord Jesus.

*The First Epistle to Timothy.* The epistles Paul sent to Timothy and Titus are personal letters. The content is largely a collection of instructions concerning ecclesiastical order, procedures, church leadership skills, and useful advice about how to select the proper leadership for the church. Paul tells Timothy that the church is the pillar and buttress of truth. Buttresses support the weight of a building. In other words, the apostle is telling us that all the faith and hope of Christ's people rest upon Him.

Paul puts the plan of salvation in a nutshell: "Without controversy great is the mystery of godliness: God was manifest in the flesh, justified in the Spirit, seen of angels, preached unto the Gentiles, believed on in the world, received up into glory" (1 Timothy 3:16). The story of Jesus, which began in heaven and ended in heaven, is the essence of the message. On earth, He was born in a little town as a human being; lived among those He came to save; taught, healed, and did all kinds of service. He was crucified without reason, rose again with the nail prints still evident, and ascended to the heavenly courts from which He had come—a blessed mystery through which those who believe find salvation! In this setting, Paul reminds us that in the person of our Lord and Savior, humanity was combined with divinity: "God was manifest in the flesh."

*The Epistle to Titus.* In the apostolic letter Paul wrote to Titus, he made a reference to Christ's divine origin that is worthy of our notice. He said that "the grace of God" teaches us that "we should live soberly, righteously, and godly, in this present world; looking for that blessed hope, and the glorious appearing of the great God and our Saviour Jesus Christ" (Titus 2:11–13).

The *New World Translation,* the version of the Bible produced by the Jehovah's Witnesses, renders the last part of this passage "while we wait for the happy hope and glorious manifestation of the great God and of [the] Savior of us, Christ Jesus" (brackets in the original). That means Two Persons are to be manifested—"the great God," and the Savior Christ Jesus.

However, Granville Sharp (1735–1813), a British abolitionist campaigner who also was a biblical scholar and a classical grammarian, pointed out what he believed to be a grammatical rule that applies in this case. He said that in the Greek New Testament, when the conjunction *and* connects two nouns, and the article *the* precedes the first noun but not the second, the second noun " 'always relates to the same person that is expressed or described by the first noun.' "[1]

In Titus 2:13, the conjunction *and* joins the nouns *God* and *Christ,** and the article *the* precedes the first noun, "God," but not the second, "Christ." The conclusion, then, is that They are One and the same. So, just as we have noted in previous passages and, indeed, can observe throughout the entire body of Pauline writings in the New Testament, Paul is telling us that Jesus Christ, whom we await in glory, is our great God as well as our Savior.

*The Epistle to the Hebrews.* The first chapter of the epistle to the Hebrews tells us that Jesus was the Creator. He is described as God's Agent who brought our world and the entire universe into existence: "God . . . hath in these last days spoken unto us by his Son, . . . by whom also he made the worlds; who being the brightness of his glory, and the express image of his person, and upholding all things by the word of his power, when he had by himself purged our sins, sat down on the right hand of the Majesty on high" (Hebrews 1:1–3).

We see that the writer of these verses realized that Jesus is more than an angel. He occupies the throne of majesty, and the angels of God worship Him. This is a clear indication that we should consider Jesus to be divine. He is God.

For unto which of the angels said he at any time, Thou art my Son, this day have I begotten thee? And again, I will be to him a Father, and he shall be to

---

*Here, the second "noun" is actually a group of nouns: "Savior Jesus Christ."

me a Son? And again, when he bringeth in the first-begotten into the world, he saith, And let all the angels of God worship him. And of the angels he saith, Who maketh his angels spirits, and his ministers a flame of fire. But unto the Son he saith, Thy throne, O God, is for ever and ever: a sceptre of righteousness is the sceptre of thy kingdom (Hebrews 1:5–8).

Here, the letter to the Hebrews again says Jesus is more than an angel. He is the Son of God and can legitimately be worshiped—which is a prerogative of God. The last verse of the passage quotes Psalm 45:6 and applies it to Jesus, the Son. In that verse, God says to the Son, "Thy throne, O God, is for ever"—a direct claim of divinity for the Son, Jesus Christ.

## Jesus in other New Testament epistles

*The second epistle of Peter.* The Granville Sharp rule applies to a line in the second epistle of Peter. The introduction to this epistle says, "Simon Peter, a servant and an apostle of Jesus Christ, to them that have obtained like precious faith with us through the righteousness of God and our Saviour Jesus Christ" (2 Peter 1:1). Again, two nouns are bridged by *kai* (the word "and"), and the article appears before the first noun and not before the second noun. Accordingly, the sentence is applying both titles to the same Person, the Lord Jesus.

*The first epistle of John.* In several places in his writings, the apostle John draws a connection between knowing Jesus and having eternal life. For instance, in his Gospel he writes,

"This is life eternal, that they might know thee the only true God, and Jesus Christ, whom thou hast sent" (John 17:3).

The apostle picks up this theme in the fifth chapter of his first epistle. Verses 18, 19, and 20 say "we know . . ." and then state a truth important to Christian believers. This series leads up to John's declaration of what Christians believe about Jesus: "And we know that the Son of God is come, and hath given us an understanding, that we may know him that is true, and we are in him that is true, even in his Son Jesus Christ. This is the true God, and eternal life" (1 John 5:20).

These words contain a weighty message. They are highly significant. They show that the apostle John doesn't have even the slightest doubt that Jesus is truly God.

## Summary

Here again are the New Testament passages that we have seen in this chapter:

- The Epistle to the Romans: "Christ came, who is over all, God blessed for ever. Amen" (Romans 9:5).
- The Epistle to the Philippians: "At the name of Jesus every knee should bow, of things in heaven, and things in earth, and things under the earth" (Philippians 2:10).
- The Epistle to the Colossians: "In him [Christ] dwelleth all the fullness of the Godhead bodily" (Colossians 2:9).
- The First Epistle to Timothy: "And without controversy great is the mystery of godliness: God was manifest in the flesh, justified in the Spirit, seen of angels, preached unto the Gentiles, believed on in

the world, received up into glory" (1 Timothy 3:16).

- The Epistle to Titus: "Looking for that blessed hope, and the glorious appearing of the great God and our Saviour Jesus Christ" (Titus 2:13).
- The Epistle to the Hebrews: "God . . . hath in these last days spoken unto us by his Son, whom he hath appointed heir of all things, by whom also he made the worlds" (Hebrews 1:1, 2).
- The second epistle of Peter: "Simon Peter, a servant and an apostle of Jesus Christ, to them that have obtained like precious faith with us through the righteousness of God and our Saviour Jesus Christ" (2 Peter 1:1).
- The first epistle of John: "And we know that the Son of God is come, . . . and we are in him that is true, even in his Son Jesus Christ. This is the true God, and eternal life" (1 John 5:20).

The evidence from this godly choir of apostles is clear; there is no other option but to believe that Jesus is God.

---

1. Granville Sharp, *Remarks on the Uses of the Definitive Article in the Greek Text of the New Testament, Containing Many New Proofs of the Divinity of Christ, from Passages Which Are Wrongly Translated in the Common English Version,* 3rd ed. (London, 1803), 3.

## Chapter 8

# Titles and Descriptives Used of Jesus

## Son of man

"Son of man" may be the title Jesus liked best. It appears more than 190 times throughout Scripture, about 80 of those times in the Gospels. In many places, it refers simply to common human beings, and it's used some 90 times in Ezekiel to designate the prophet. However, there is also a detectable Messianic undertone in some instances where the term appears in Scripture. In the book of Daniel, for example, in the setting of a scene of judgment, it designates a mysterious Personage close to the Ancient of Days.

| Old Testament | Attributes | New Testament |
| --- | --- | --- |
| "I saw in the night visions, and, behold, one like the Son of man came with the clouds of heaven, and came to the Ancient of days, and they brought him near before him" (Daniel 7: 13). | Heavenly attributes<br>Majesty<br>Judgment | "And then shall appear the sign of the Son of man in heaven: and then shall all the tribes of the earth mourn, and they shall see the Son of man coming in the clouds of heaven with power and great glory" (Matthew 24:30). "Jesus saith unto him, Thou hast said: nevertheless I say unto you, Hereafter shall ye see the Son of man sitting on the right hand of power, and coming in the clouds of heaven" (Matthew 26:64). |

The title *Son of man* primarily and most commonly serves simply to designate a being who has human nature. On a secondary level and more focused level, the Lord uses the term of His prophets, such as Ezekiel. And on a third and ultimate level, the term is used in the context of the judgment prophesied for the end time, when a heavenly Being who bears this title will carry out the function of Judge. It is in this eschatological context that Jesus used the expression and applied it to His own person.

## Michael

The name *Michael* comes from the Hebrew *Mikha'el*. It means "Who is like God." Talmudic tradition regarded this as a rhetorical question "Who is like God?" meant to be answered "No one." Several common people in the Bible bore the name Michael, but so did a heavenly Being who appears in eschatological passages of the Bible. Among those passages are the following:

- "The prince of the kingdom of Persia withstood me one and twenty days: but, lo, Michael, one of the chief princes, came to help me" (Daniel 10:13).
- "There is none that holdeth with me in these things, but Michael your prince" (verse 21).
- "At that time shall Michael stand up, the great prince which standeth for the children of thy people: and there shall be a time of trouble, such as never was since there was a nation even to that same time: and at that time thy people shall be delivered, every one that shall be found written in the book" (Daniel 12:1).

- "Michael the archangel, when contending with the devil he disputed about the body of Moses, durst not bring against him a railing accusation, but said, The Lord rebuke thee" (Jude 9).
- "There was war in heaven: Michael and his angels fought against the dragon; and the dragon fought and his angels" (Revelation 12:7).

So, who is this Michael?

As we've seen, His name means "[One] who is like God."

He appears as an Archangel—and at His second advent, Jesus comes "with the voice of the archangel" (1 Thessalonians 4:16).

He battles against Satan; during His earthly life and ministry, Jesus was in constant conflict with Satan. Jesus also said, "I beheld Satan as lightning fall from heaven" (Luke 10:18).

He will appear at the end of time.

These biblical references don't tell us directly who Michael is. But perhaps they also point to the Person we find in the meaning of the name. After all, isn't Jesus the only One who *really* is like God?

### Wisdom personified

Debates concerning Jesus' origin often focus on a portion of Scripture found in the book of Proverbs, in a section that we may call the personification of wisdom.

> The Lord possessed me in the beginning of his way, before his works of old. I was set up from everlasting, from the beginning, or ever the earth was. When there were no depths, I was brought forth;

when there were no fountains abounding with water. Before the mountains were settled, before the
hills was I brought forth: while as yet he had not
made the earth, nor the fields, nor the highest part
of the dust of the world. When he prepared the
heavens, I was there: when he set a compass upon
the face of the depth (Proverbs 8:22–27).

What connections can we establish between Proverbs 8
and the Lord Jesus?

Let's be clear from the start: the argument that Proverbs
8 implies that Jesus had a beginning is not supported by the
hermeneutical principles that give dependable guidance to
our interpretation of Scripture. Wisdom literature and po-
etical literature often employ figurative language that generally is not considered to provide a sound foundation for es-
tablishing doctrine.

There are several factors to which we must pay close attention if we are to understand this passage correctly: the book of
Proverbs is classed as wisdom literature; wisdom literature has
definitive characteristics; the "wisdom of God" conforms to a
particular biblical context; and the passage in Proverbs that
speaks of wisdom doesn't make a direct reference to any person.

In Scripture, wisdom literature is a form that is compa-
rable to but differs from prophetic and liturgical literature
and law. Wisdom literature's primary concern is with general ethical and religious topics, of which it speaks in a re-
flective tone. Job, Psalms, Proverbs, Song of Solomon, and
Ecclesiastes compose the books generally classed as wisdom
literature. Jesus and the apostles recognized this portion of
Scripture as divinely inspired. Wisdom literature character-

istically emphasizes practical matters, Creation theology, and strong dependence on God.

The writers of wisdom literature used different forms: proverbs, sayings, riddles, admonitions, allegories, hymns and prayers, dialogues, confessions, onomastica, and beatitudes.[1]

To interpret wisdom literature correctly, one needs to take into account the particular literary form the writer was using, the general orientation of the book, and the context. Considering an individual statement to be the whole truth on a subject skews one's interpretation.

Both the Old and the New Testaments contain references to the "wisdom of God." (See, for example, 1 Kings 3:28; Luke 11:49; 1 Corinthians 1:21, 24; 2:7; and Ephesians 3:10.) It is interesting that in Luke 11:49, the expression seems to be used as synonymous with God, a concept that may be in agreement with the general worldview and also with the religious vision of the Hebrew people.

In general, we may say that certain concepts characteristic of wisdom serve as the building blocks of Proverbs. These are that God is the Source of wisdom (Proverbs 2:6); wisdom was instrumental in Creation (Proverbs 3:19); and wisdom is to be valued (Proverbs 5:5–8; 8:11).

Our understanding of wisdom would not be complete without a couple of caveats. First, Proverbs 8 doesn't support the idea that wisdom is subordinated to the Lord; one must misunderstand the texts to see such a tension there. Instead, the texts reveal that wisdom and the Lord have always existed in harmony.[2]

In fact, 1 Corinthians 1:30 says that God has made Jesus to be our wisdom. Aside from this, there is no direct connection between Jesus and Proverbs 8. No New Testament writer makes such a connection.

On the other hand, the Creator is not without wisdom, nor does wisdom exist without the Creator. Applying a kind of surgical interpretation that separates wisdom from God may imply that there was a time when God finally got around to creating wisdom. If that were true, then there must have been a time when God was devoid of wisdom! That would certainly be an irreverent misuse of the biblical text and hardly the sort of message intended by Solomon in the Proverbs. Would it not be a far more consistent and reasonable view of this passage to understand it as saying that in timeless eternity before this world came into existence, wisdom was with God, and that wisdom was displayed in all His wonderful works of creation? Common sense tells us that wisdom is as eternal as God Himself.

## The Only Begotten

In the New Testament, two terms are applied to Jesus that might challenge our understanding: "only begotten" (*monogenēs*) and "firstborn" (*prōtotokos*). Some people conclude that these terms mean that Jesus must have been derived from or must have "proceeded" from God, and that would make Jesus a lesser being than the Eternal Father.

"Only begotten" is a translation of the Greek word *monogenēs,* an adjective that is a combination of two words: *monos,* "one" or "only," and *ginomai,* "to become" or "to be." Louw and Nida define *monogenēs* as "pertaining to what is unique in the sense of being the only one of the same kind or class."[3] And the *Theological Dictionary of the New Testament* says, "*Monogenēs* is used for the only child. More generally it means 'unique' or 'incomparable.' "[4]

Clement of Rome used the word that way. In his first letter to the Corinthians, writing of a mythological bird whose origins were unknown , he said, "This, being [is] the only one of its kind"—*monogenēs.*[5]

Paul must have had this meaning in mind when he wrote in Hebrews 11:17, "By faith Abraham, when he was tried, offered up Isaac: and he that had received the promises offered up his only begotten [*monogenēs*] son." Louw and Nida comment on this: "Abraham, of course, did have another son, Ishmael, and later sons by Keturah, but Isaac was a unique son in that he was a son born as the result of certain promises made by God. Accordingly, he could be called a [*monogenēs*] son, since he was the only one of his kind."[6]

These examples make it apparent that when "only begotten" is applied to Jesus, the emphasis is not on His origin but rather on His uniqueness—that He is special, with no equal, incomparable, one of a kind.

## Firstborn

Paul is the one who applies to Jesus the second difficult term mentioned above: "firstborn" (Greek: *prōtotokos*). Literally, the term means the firstborn offspring of either humans or animals. But as is true of all other languages, Greek words can have a figurative or symbolic meaning as well as a literal meaning. When used figuratively, to be *prōtotokos* means to be preeminent in rank, status, or position—to be elected, separate from others, favored, or distinguished above others.

In the Bible, David is called "firstborn" although he was actually the youngest of Jesse's eight sons (Psalm 89:20–27). And Israel is described as firstborn although it was by no means the first nation on earth (Exodus 4:22). Israel was the firstborn in the sense of being chosen or "elected" by God. It's in this sense that this title is applied to Jesus in the New Testament (Colossians 1:18; Hebrews 1:6; Revelation 1:5).

## The beginning of the Creation of God

The book of Revelation contains an expression that some people have misinterpreted: "And unto the angel of the church of the Laodiceans write; These things saith the Amen, the faithful and true witness, *the beginning of the creation of God*" (Revelation 3:14; emphasis added). Readers without any biblical background might easily conclude that this verse means that Jesus is a created being. But to understand the meaning of this phrase, we must take into account, first, Jesus' relationship to Creation; and second, how the term *beginning* is used in the book of Revelation.

Regarding Jesus' relationship to Creation, John makes it clear in his Gospel that Jesus was the active Agent in Creation. Jesus wasn't *created*—He was the *Creator*. "In the beginning was the Word, and the Word was with God, and the Word was God. . . . All things were made by him; and without him was not any thing made that was made" (John 1:1, 3).

Notice that to make the point as clear and as impregnable as he could, John wrote it in two ways—one positive and one negative. Writing in the positive, John said Jesus made *everything*—"all things." And writing in the negative, he said nothing that was created was made by anyone else; no one else brought anything that didn't exist into existence. So, Jesus was the causative force at work in Creation. To say that in any of the writings of John—the Gospel, epistles, or Revelation—he considers Jesus to be a created being is to reveal a total misunderstanding of John's fundamental message.

As to the second point, John used the Greek word *archē*, "beginning," in Revelation 21:6 as well as in Revelation 3:14. In Revelation 21:6, the word applies to God; He is "the beginning and the end"—an indisputable reference to His eternal existence. (Compare what God declared centuries earlier through the prophet Isaiah: "I am the first, I also am the last" [Isaiah 48:12].) Jesus isn't the beginning in the sense that He *had* a beginning, but in the sense that He *began* all things that exist—all things had their beginning in Him.

So, in each of his New Testament works, concluding with Revelation, the apostle John demonstrated singularity of purpose. In all he wrote, he aimed to present Jesus Christ as truly God.

1. Grant R. Osborne, *The Hermeneutical Spiral: A Comprehensive Introduction to Biblical Interpretation* (Downers Grove, Ill.: IVP Academic, 2006), 247–250.

2. Richard M. Davidson, "Proverbs 8 and the Place of Christ in the Trinity," *Journal of the Adventist Theological Society* 17, no. 1 (Spring 2006): 33–54.

3. Johannes P. Louw and Eugene A. Nida, eds., *Greek-English Lexicon of the New Testament Based on Semantic Domains,* 2nd ed. (New York: United Bible Societies, 1989), 1:591.

4. Geoffrey Bromiley, *Theological Dictionary of the New Testament,* eds. Gerhard Kittel and Gerhard Friedrich (Grand Rapids, Mich.: Eerdmans, 1985), 607.

5. Clement of Rome, *Ante-Nicene Fathers,* chapter 25; quoted in Richard Longenecker, "The One and Only Son," *The NIV: The Making of a Contemporary Translation* (Colorado Springs, Colo.: International Bible Society, 1991), 122. For his quotation of this passage from 1 Clement, Longenecker used J. B. Lightfoot's translation (without attribution), with only a few changes for the sake of modern English.

6. Louw and Nida, eds., *Greek-English Lexicon,* 1:591.

# Chapter 9
# The Holy Spirit

The Old Testament mentions the Holy Spirit, and we see more of Him in the New Testament. In an article titled "Reflections on the Doctrine of the Trinity," Raoul Dederen wrote, "In the OT the expression *ruach qôdesh* occurs only three times and even then with 'thine' or 'his,' whereas in the NT, the Holy Spirit (*pneuma hagion*) occurs 88 times, sometimes with the definite article and sometimes without it."[1]

Jesus promised the coming of the Holy Spirit, and the apostles made repeated references to Him. Is the Holy Spirit a Person? Is He divine?

Jesus said, "Go ye therefore, and teach all nations, baptizing them in the name of the Father, and of the Son, and of the Holy Ghost" (Matthew 28:19). Clearly, the Holy Spirit is an integral part of the "name" (singular) in which we are baptized. Those who deny the personhood of the Holy Spirit are at odds with this text and must then face the resultant inconsistencies regarding the other Two Persons who bear this name. They end up wresting Scripture, weakening credence in the verse's intent, and are obliged to re-write the Bible to conform to their unsustainable interpretations.

## Is the Holy Spirit a Person?

Some religious movements claim that the Holy Spirit isn't a Member of the Godhead. They think Him to be some kind of "active force" or "divine afflatus" that emanates from God. But notice how Scripture refers to the Holy Spirit: "When the Comforter is come, . . . even the Spirit of truth, which proceedeth from the Father, *he* shall testify of me" (John 15:26; emphasis added).* Divine afflatuses are not referred to with personal pronouns such as *he* or *she,* but with an impersonal *it.* The fact that Scripture uses personal pronouns to refer to the Holy Spirit is strong evidence that He is a personal Being, not a thing.

Scripture also ascribes the characteristics of a person to the Holy Spirit. It indicates the following:

> *The Holy Spirit has a mind.* "He that searcheth the hearts knoweth what is the mind of the Spirit, because he maketh intercession for the saints according to the will of God" (Romans 8:27).
>
> *The Holy Spirit has an individual will.* He withheld permission for Paul, Silas, and Timothy to go into Bithynia (Acts 16:7, 8). And Paul wrote that He has given "gifts" to the church according to His will (1 Corinthians 12:7–11).
>
> *The Holy Spirit gives instructions and knows the future.* "The Spirit speaketh expressly, that in the latter times some shall depart from the faith, giving heed to seducing spirits, and doctrines of devils" (1 Timothy 4:1). "The Holy Ghost shall teach you in the same hour what ye ought to say" (Luke 12:12).

Scripture also says the Holy Spirit can be blasphemed

---

*John says "*he* shall testify," *ekeinos*—a demonstrative pronoun that is a nominative masculine singular.

against (Matthew 12:31, 32), tested (Acts 5:9), resisted (Acts 7:51; 1 Thessalonians 5:19), and grieved (Ephesians 4:30). These are things that can only be said of beings who are persons.

*The Holy Spirit has divine attributes.* Scripture reveals that the Holy Spirit has attributes exclusively reserved by God; for example, His omnipresence, eternal existence, and His power to create.

The psalmist attributes omnipresence to the Holy Spirit, and so does Luke, the author of Acts. David asked, "Whither shall I go from thy spirit? or whither shall I flee from thy presence?" (Psalm 139:7). And quoting the Old Testament, Luke wrote, "It shall come to pass in the last days, saith God, I will pour out my Spirit upon all flesh: and your sons and your daughters shall prophesy, and your young men shall see visions, and your old men shall dream dreams" (Acts 2:17).

The author of Hebrews calls the Holy Spirit "eternal." He says that if the blood of sacrificial animals makes people outwardly clean, then "how much more shall the blood of Christ, who through *the eternal Spirit* offered himself without spot to God, purge your conscience from dead works to serve the living God?" (Hebrews 9:14; emphasis added).

Genesis 1 pictures the "Spirit of God" moving upon earth's waters when God began to create (verse 2). And the book of Job reports Elihu's words, "The Spirit of God hath made me, and the breath of the Almighty hath given me life" (Job 33:4).

According to Jesus, the Holy Spirit also is active in the re-creation of each one who accepts Him: "Except a man be born of water and of the Spirit, he cannot enter into the kingdom of God. . . . The wind bloweth where it listeth, and thou hearest the sound thereof, but canst not tell whence it cometh, and whither it goeth: so is every one that is born of the Spirit" (John 3:5, 8).

*Bible writers interchange the names of God and the Holy Spirit.* The apostle Paul, for instance, equates the human "temples of God" with the "temples of the Holy Spirit."

| Referring to God | Referring to the Holy Spirit |
|---|---|
| "Know ye not that ye are the temple of God" (1 Corinthians 3:16). | "Know ye not that your body is the temple of the Holy Ghost" (1 Corinthians 6:19). |

*To lie to the Holy Spirit is to lie to God.* Acts 5 presents the case of Ananias and Sapphira. They attempted to short-change the Holy Spirit, and when the apostles gave them the opportunity to tell the truth, they both persisted in their lies. In his comments about their actions, Peter makes it perfectly clear that cheating the Spirit is the same thing as cheating God.

| Lied to the Holy Spirit | Lied to God |
|---|---|
| "Why hath Satan filled thine heart to lie to the Holy Ghost" (Acts 5:3). | "Thou hast not lied unto men, but unto God" (Acts 5:4). |

*In the Bible, the Holy Spirit is referred to as Lord.* The Epistle to the Hebrews contains a quotation from the Old Testament that says, "The Holy Ghost also is a witness to us: for . . . he had said before, This is the covenant that I will make with them after those days, saith the Lord, I will put my laws into their hearts, and in their minds will I write them" (Hebrews 10:15, 16).

Verse 16 is a quotation from the book of Jeremiah: "This shall be the covenant that I will make with the house of Israel; After those days, saith the LORD, I will put my law in their inward parts, and write it in their hearts; and will be their God, and they shall be my people" (Jeremiah 31:33). Significantly, what Jeremiah says the Lord has spoken is, in the Epistle to the Hebrews, ascribed to the Holy Spirit. So, we can conclude that in the Epistle to the Hebrews, the Holy Spirit, in both name and person, corresponds to *YHWH*—to the Lord.

This text supports the idea that the apostle believed the Holy Spirit to be of the same rank as Jeremiah's Lord—*YHWH*, in other words. The logical conclusion, then, is that this was the accepted understanding in the early Christian church. They believed the Holy Spirit and the Lord of Scripture to be Members of the Godhead of equal standing.

*The Holy Spirit shared with God and Jesus key moments in the history of salvation.* As we have previously noted, the Holy Spirit was present with the Father and the Son at Creation. The Spirit and the Father also revealed Their presence at Jesus' baptism. Luke renders the event this way: "The Holy Ghost descended in a bodily shape like a dove upon him [Jesus], and a voice came from heaven, which said, Thou art my beloved Son; in thee I am well pleased" (Luke 3:22).

*The Holy Spirit was the Source of prophecy.* "For the prophecy came not in old time by the will of man: but holy men of God spake as they were moved by the Holy Ghost" (2 Peter 1:21).

*The Holy Spirit made His presence known at Pentecost.*

Jesus promised His disciples the coming of the Holy Spirit. "Ye shall receive power, after that the Holy Ghost is come upon you: and ye shall be witnesses unto me both in Jerusalem, and in all Judaea, and in Samaria, and unto the uttermost part of the earth" (Acts 1:8). That empowering from the Holy Spirit began the grand missionary outreach to the world.

## Summary

In this chapter we have explored several aspects of the Holy Spirit. Faithful to the consistent testimony of Scripture as it is, our understanding of the Holy Spirit as a personal Being who is a full Member of the Godhead stands as firmly grounded truth. We arrived at this position from what is evident in the biblical narrative throughout both the Old and the New Testaments. The Holy Spirit appears in a prehuman and metahuman level. Scripture clearly portrays His role as on a plane far superior to that of the angels. He is united with and equal to the Father and Jesus Christ, the Son. This body of facts offers us solid reasons to include Him among the Personages of the Godhead.

The ascended Jesus provided the Spirit as His personal Substitute. That fact tells us that the Spirit is a personal Being. No ethereal notion or wafting thing could adequately fill the place of the ascended Jesus; only a Divine Person who knows Jesus intimately—who can represent Him and ingrain His teachings—can satisfactorily replace Him.

The Holy Spirit was the active Agent in Creation. He was the channel through which Jesus was miraculously conceived in human flesh. He revealed Himself in visible form at Jesus' baptism, and He inundated the early church with

His presence. The book of Acts portrays the Holy Spirit as the foremost of Divine Intercessors in the work of growing God's fledgling church. He speaks. He hears. He calls. He commands. He sends. He intercedes. He is always present. And the apostles recognize Him as existing and working on a par with the heavenly Father and their risen Lord Jesus, the Son of God. Let us then offer Him, too, our worship and praise!

---

1. Raoul Dederen, "Reflections on the Doctrine of the Trinity," 8.

# Chapter 10
# Twisted Concepts of God

To have an informed understanding of the tri-unity, we must review other explanations of the Godhead. What follows is an alphabetized and annotated listing of the principal examples of those that are considered heretical.

## Adoptionism

Those who hold the view of adoptionism consider Jesus to be a man gifted with extraordinary powers, who was then "adopted" by God at His baptism when the Father proclaimed, "This is my beloved Son" (Matthew 3:17).

## Apollinarianism

According to Apollinarius of Laodicea (c. A.D. 310–390), Jesus' body was human, but the divine *Logos* took possession of His mind, so He had a divine mind, not a human one. This concept diminishes the humanity of Jesus in favor of His divinity.

## Arianism

Arius (c. A.D. 250–336), a Christian patriarch from Alexandria, Egypt, denied that Jesus was fully God. In his view, Jesus hadn't existed throughout eternity past; He was created at some point and for that reason should be classed below God the Father. Arius also held that the Holy Spirit was not a person; rather, the Holy Spirit was an active force that emanated from God. The Jehovah's Witnesses' understanding of Jesus comes close to that of Arius.

## Binitarianism

Those who hold the position of binitarianism believe that there are only Two Persons in the Godhead. Some of them deny the divinity of Jesus, and others the divinity of the Holy Spirit. Herbert W. Armstrong's movement embraced this position, and the Reorganized Church of Jesus Christ (an offshoot of Mormonism) holds a view that closely resembles it.

## Docetism

The name of *docetism* comes from the Greek word *dokeo,* "to seem." Those who hold this position believe that what appeared to be the physical body of Jesus was an illusion. They believe that His essence was ethereal, pure spirit, and consequently, Jesus couldn't die physically. John 1:14, then, becomes merely figurative.

## Modalism

The perspective of modalism is also called Sabellianism. Its followers believe that God can appear in any one of three different modes or roles: sometimes as the Father, sometimes as the Son, and sometimes as the Holy Spirit. There are variations of this position, one of which is called Oneness (see below).

## Monophysitism

The term *monophysitism* comes from the Greek words *monos,* "one," and *physis,* "nature." Basically, it argues that Christ has only one nature—His divine nature—because His humanity has been fully absorbed by His divinity.

## Monothelitism

The name *monothelitism* comes from *monos,* "one," and *thelēma,* "will," and means "one will." This Christological position appeared in Armenia and Syria. It purported that while Jesus had two natures—human and divine—He had only one will.

Of course, this clashes with Scripture. In Gethsemane, Jesus prayed, "O my Father, if it be possible, let this cup pass from me: nevertheless not as I will, but as thou wilt" (Matthew 26:39).

## Nestorianism

Nestorious, a patriarch of the Christian church who lived in Constantinople in the fifth century A.D., agreed that Jesus did, indeed, have two natures, divine and human, which is orthodox thinking. But he added that Jesus was manifested in Two Persons. The drawback comes at the atonement: if Jesus was Two Persons, which One died at the cross?

## Oneness / Oneness Pentecostalism

Oneness, or Oneness Pentecostalism, is a religious movement close to Pentecostal Christianity that, however, doesn't accept the doctrine of the Trinity. Adherents support what has been termed the Oneness doctrine, which "states that there is one God, a singular spirit who manifests himself in many different ways, including as Father, Son and Holy Spirit."[1] They argue, " 'If there is only one God and that God is the Father (Mal. 2:10), and if Jesus is God, then it logically follows that Jesus is the Father.' "[2]

## Patripassianism

The name *patripassianism* is derived from a combination of two Latin words: *patri,* "father," and *passio,* "suffer," and it means "the Father suffers." Those who hold this position believe that God the Father was incarnated in Jesus, and He suffered on the cross together with Jesus. But the orthodox Christian understanding of the Crucifixion is that the divine nature of Christ neither suffered nor died.

## Subordinationism

To be subordinate means to be subject to or placed under the authority of a superior. Subordinationists insist that the Son is subject to the Father in nature but not in function. Justin Martyr (c. A.D. 100–165), Origen (A.D. 185–254), and several other pre-Nicean writers may be considered to have voiced this position in their writings.

## Tritheism

Those who hold the position of tritheism argue that there are three distinct Gods. This position has very little to do with the doctrine of the Trinity as generally conceived. It is because of tritheism that some non-Christians consider Christians to be polytheists. A few authors have suggested that the Seventh-day Adventist Church has embraced tritheisim.[3] This little book should make it clear that such is hardly the case.

## Summary

From the point of view of the author of this study, serious problems arise when people depend on their finite human reasoning to understand the nature of God. That leads only to twisted notions that produce freakish, man-made gods. Instead, we must let the Bible speak for itself concerning God. The vision of Scripture remains clearest when we don't clutter it with too much philosophizing. There is a lesson to be learned from the fact that the authors of the Bible did not feel it necessary to clear up every divine mystery.

The Bible presents the One and only God. The Hebrew Scriptures point to plurality within the Godhead, yet the Scriptures also consistently refer to God as One. The New Testament provides names for the Members of the Godhead: the Father, the Son, and the Holy Spirit. But even though the New Testament gives us those three names (plural), it still specifies that believers are to be baptized "in the name" (singular), not "in the names" (plural) of the Father, Son, and Holy Spirit.

We must consider the Word of God to be its own expositor. Let the Bible inspire our faith; it will do a far better job of that than nit-picking or second-guessing divine mysteries ever can.

---

1. "Oneness Pentecostalism," Wikipedia, accessed May 25, 2011, http://en.wikipedia.org/wiki/Oneness_Pentecostalism.

2. David Bernard, *The Oneness of God,* vol. 1 of Series in Pentecostal Theology (Hazelwood, Mo.: Word Aflame Press, 1983), 66; quoted in Gregory A. Boyd, *Oneness Pentecostalism and the Trinity: A World-Wide Movement Assessed by a Former Oneness Pentecostal* (Grand Rapids, Mich.: Baker Books, 1992), 28.

3. "Tritheism," Wikipedia, accessed May 25, 2011, http://en.wikipedia.org/wiki/Tritheism.

# Chapter 11

# Questions and Answers

### Q: Is the word *trinity* used in the Bible?

**A:** No, the word *trinity* is not used in either the Old Testament or the New Testament. Some expressions need time to flourish. Joseph and Mary probably never called their Divine Son *Jesus Christ,* but there is no doubt that the infant Christian church fully understood and accepted that name. The name *Christian* wasn't used during the earliest years of the church either; believers most often referred to themselves as those who belong to "the way" (Acts 9:2; 22:4; 24:22). Names and terms such as *trinity,* then, are creations inspired by their usefulness. The vital point is that believers should be sure these creative terms conform to and harmonize with Scripture. The word *trinity* serves a good purpose in that it refers to Three Persons—the Father, the Son, and the Holy Spirit—who comprise only One God.

### Q: Are there other expressions with which to describe this unity of God?

**A:** People quite commonly use the biblical expression *Godhead* (Colossians 2:9) and the word *tri-unity.*

### Q: Was Ellen G. White supportive of the concept of the tri-unity of God?

**A:** There is evidence in her writings that she believed in the tri-unity of God.

"There are three living person of the heavenly trio;

in the name of these three great powers—the Father, the Son, and the Holy Spirit—those who receive Christ by living faith are baptized."[1]

"In Christ is life, original, unborrowed, underived. 'He that hath the Son hath life.' . . . The divinity of Christ is the believer's assurance of eternal life."[2]

"Sin could be resisted and overcome only through the mighty agency of the Third Person of the Godhead, who would come with no modified energy, but in the fullness of divine power. It is the Spirit that makes effectual what has been wrought out by the world's Redeemer."[3]

The writings of Ellen White regarding the tri-unity of God are sound and clear. Her writings on this topic and our convictions as Seventh-day Adventists regarding the Godhead are based solely upon the evidence that comes from Scripture.

### Q: Have people changed what Ellen White wrote about the Trinity?

**A:** Tim Poirier wrote an excellent article titled "Ellen White's Trinitarian Statements: What Did She Actually Write?" in which he used manuscripts in Ellen White's own handwriting to demonstrate that she was indeed responsible for the statements that some people have questioned.[4]

### Q: Is the Adventist understanding of the Trinity the same as that held by Roman Catholics?

**A:** No, it is not. There is a major difference between the

Roman Catholic and the Seventh-day Adventist views of the Trinity. Catholicism looks to the authority of the *magisterium,* "the living teaching office of the church."[5] The catechism presents a long and complex definition that states that the Son is "begotten not made"[6] and goes on to say that "since the Father has through generation given the only-begotten Son everything that belongs to the Father, except being Father, the Son has also eternally from the Father, from whom he is eternally born, that the Holy Spirit proceeds from the Son."[7] In summary, the Catholic Church teaches that the Holy Spirit proceeds from the Son and the Son from the Father. This concept doesn't come from the Bible and isn't a teaching of the Seventh-day Adventist Church.

**Q: The pioneers of the Seventh-day Adventist Church didn't believe in the tri-unity of God. How then can we follow this doctrine?**

**A:** No doubt some Adventists find this question shocking. The answer might prove to be equally shocking, so let's calmly look at the following facts from our church's history.

1. All our pioneers belonged to other denominations before they became Seventh-day Adventists.
2. A significant number of them came from the Christian Connection.
3. The twenty-eight fundamental beliefs didn't already exist when the Seventh-day Adventist Church was born.
4. Extrapolating from these facts, we can see how extra "baggage" might have been (and was) brought into

Adventism along with the truths that the pioneers brought with them. Subsequently, through timely study, old misconceptions were replaced with better, more biblical positions.

5. Sound evidence from Ellen White's writings shows us that the doctrine of the Trinity is the correct understanding of the Godhead.

*1. All our pioneers belonged to other denominations before they became Seventh-day Adventists.* Ellen G. White was baptized as a Methodist. (Her father served as a deacon in that church.) Ellen and her parents transitioned into the Millerite movement before Seventh-day Adventism even existed. James White was baptized and ordained to the ministry in the Christian Connection. John Nevins Andrews, a Millerite who became an Adventist and even served as president of the Adventist Church and as its first official overseas missionary, was a fervent anti-Trinitarian. Joseph Bates, another influential pioneer, wrote in 1868, "Respecting the trinity, I concluded that it was an impossibility for me to believe that the Lord Jesus Christ, the Son of the Father, was also the Almighty God, the Father, one and the same being."[8] In answering a question on the topic, J. N. Loughborough said, "There are many objections which we might urge, but on account of our limited space we shall reduce them to the three following: 1. It is contrary to common sense. 2. It is contrary to scripture. 3. Its origin is Pagan and fabulous."[9] Uriah Smith became a Sabbath keeper in 1852. He was an outstanding leader and writer of the Seventh-day Adventist Church, but he did not accept the doctrine of the Trinity. He called Christ the "first created being."[10]

Jerry Moon, professor of church history at the seminary at Andrews University, says development of the Trinity concept among Seventh-day Adventists advanced through five stages: (1) anti-Trinitarian dominance (1846–1888); (2) beginnings of dissatisfaction with anti-Trinitarianism (1888–1898); (3) paradigm shift (1898–1915); (4) decline of anti-Trinitarianism (1915–1946); and (5) Trinitarian dominance (1946 to the present).[11]

What was the turning point for this doctrine? The majority of thinkers and writers in the church consider the publication of Ellen White's book *The Desire of Ages* to be the turning point.

*2. A significant number of our influential pioneers came from the Christian Connection.* The Christian Connection was "a loose-knit confederation of churches that represented perhaps the first indigenous religious movement in America. As a rule they were suspicious of organized religion and encouraged members to take religious destiny into their own hands and to think for themselves. While they were tenacious in their own beliefs, they did not force their beliefs on others; rather, they were willing to give every man the utmost freedom of thought and expression."[12]

*3. The twenty-eight fundamental beliefs didn't already exist when the Seventh-day Adventist Church was born.* Quite reasonably, those fundamental beliefs had to develop over a period of years. Even when this writer became a member back in the 1960s, the church hadn't yet arrived at all of those twenty-eight fundamental beliefs.

When the church was in its infancy, there were perhaps only two principal doctrines regarding everyone accept— the soon return of the Lord, and the continuing validity of the seventh-day Sabbath. The church, of course, had held the doctrines of the sanctuary and the prophecies about the time of the end from very early on; however, our understanding of them was still developing. And all of our other doctrines were still in the incubating process, awaiting their due date. We hadn't yet received light on the health message, so vegetarianism and the distinction between "clean" and "unclean" meats meant practically nothing. But commendably, there was a lively spirit among those searchers for truth; they were willing to change their beliefs to accord with whatever they might find in Scripture.

*4. Extrapolating from these facts, we can see how extra "baggage" might have been (and was) brought into Adventism along with the truths that the pioneers brought with them. Subsequently, through timely study, old misconceptions were replaced with better, more biblical positions.* When Divine Providence and careful Bible study intertwine, the change that inevitably accompanies growth in our understanding takes place. Our knowledge of geography has advanced tremendously beyond what the Old Testament sages knew. Our faith and our knowledge of God's Word and His will should advance too. It has in the past. The Reformation made great strides forward as people's understanding of Scripture grew. Protestantism, while fragmented and often hard pressed from within and from without, prospered spiritually as it advanced toward greater spiritual light. Adventism must experience a similar pattern of unfolding spiritual and biblical growth.

In chapter 1, I quoted from a piece I wrote a half paragraph that delineated the loss of important doctrines in the centuries that followed the death of the first Christians.

That paragraph went on to say the following:

> Those lost values experienced a degree of rebirth
> during the Protestant Reformation (1517)—*By
> Faith Alone, Sovereign Grace, Scripture and only
> Scripture*—, and what Protestantism left only par-
> tially accomplished the rising Adventist Church
> would complete, *i.e.*: continued validity of God's
> Law, the Sabbath, the nature of man, Bible prophe-
> cies, biblical baptism, the Lord's Supper, the health
> message, the second coming, the millennium, the
> heavenly sanctuary ministry of Christ, the great
> controversy between good and evil, the spirit of
> prophecy, etc.[13]

*5. Sound evidence from Ellen White's writings shows us that
the doctrine of the Trinity is the correct understanding of the
Godhead.* As we have seen, the Trinitarian concept has developed over a period of time, as have other doctrines of the
Seventh-day Adventist Church. Ellen White's ministry
spanned the transitions that the Adventist Church experi-
enced in the nineteenth and early twentieth century. She
was a major spiritual presence in the church during the
anti-Trinitarian period (1846–1888), she continued her
counsels during the beginning of dissatisfaction with anti-
Trinitarianism (1888–1898), she was part of the paradigm
shift regarding the Trinity (1898–1915), and she died at the
beginning of the decline of anti-Trinitarianism. These historical developments were providential advances in our de-
nominational journey towards the recovery of the pure doctrine of God as it is presented in Scripture.

## Summary

I must say that because of some of the doctrinal positions a few of our pioneers espoused, it seems doubtful to me that our church today would be very willing to accept them into membership. On the other hand, it is quite possible that if they were alive today, some of our doctrinal positions would be equally unacceptable to them. What does this teach us if not that we must all understand that faith is a journey and it is prayerful study of Scripture that moves us along?

While we hold our pioneers in high esteem, believing exactly what—and only what—they did isn't a standard we should accept. None of us can see or receive *all* of the light God has for His people at a given stage of history. Let us strive—yet without strife—to be in harmony with the Bible. Surely that is what the Spirit promotes in every honest heart as He leads His people forward.

1. Ellen G. White, *Special Testimonies,* Series B, no. 7, 63.

2. Ellen G. White, *The Desire of Ages* (Mountain View, Calif.: Pacific Press®, 1940), 530.

3. Ibid., 671.

4. Tim Poirier, "Ellen White's Trinitarian Statements: What Did She Actually Write?" *"Ellen White and Current Issues" Symposium* (2006): 18–40. See www.whiteestate.org/issues/The-Trinity.pdf.

5. *Catechism of the Catholic Church*, 2nd ed. (Rome: Libreria Editrice Vaticana, 1997), 887.

6. Ibid., 64.

7. Ibid., 65.

8. Joseph Bates, *The Autobiography of Elder Joseph Bate*s (Battle Creek, Mich.: Steam Press of the Seventh-day Adventist Publishing Association, 1868), 205.

9. J. N. Loughborough, "Questions for Bro. Loughborough," *Review and Herald,* November 5, 1861, 184.

10. Uriah Smith, *Thoughts, Critical and Practical, on the Book of Rev-*

*elation* (Battle Creek, Mich.: Steam Press of the Seventh-day Adventist Publishing Association, 1865), 59.

11. W. Whidden, J. Moon, and J. Reeve, *The Trinity: Understanding God's Love, His Plan of Salvation, and Christian Relationships* (Hagerstown, Md.: Review and Herald®, 2002), 190–200.

12. Mark Ford, *The Church at Washington, New Hampshire: Discovering the Roots of Adventism* (Hagerstown, Md.: Review and Herald®, 2002), 18. See also Ronald L. Numbers and Jonathan M. Butler, eds., *The Disappointment* (Indianapolis: Indiana University Press, 1987), 222, 223; and Francis D. Nichol, *The Midnight Cry* (Washington D.C.: Review and Herald®, 1944), 274, 275.

13. Daniel Scarone, "Why Are General Conference Sessions Held?" Adventist Pastor Online, http://www.adventistpastoronline.com/index .php/why-are-general-conference-sessions-held.

# Chapter 12
# Conclusion

Attempting to understand the doctrine of God is perhaps the most daunting of quests. Just how much can an ant discover about elephants? The possibility of our puny minds coming up with anything lucid concerning the Godhead might seem about that remote! Nevertheless, if we put our sanctified minds to work, we should be able to reach some valuable conclusions about this Eternal Being who created life and has said He wants us to know Him.

One thing stands out to me about this pursuit: the wisdom of sticking very close to Scripture, for it is God's testimony, which He intends to guide serious, open-minded folks into a truly worthwhile understanding of divine science. It is humbling to realize that in considerations such as this, though we today have amazing tools at our disposition, there always has been a fairly level playing field over the millennia of history. For God generously gives to every generation opportunities to walk and talk with Him. Our questions and His answers compose a living dynamic of unending exchange. To know Him more perfectly is the quest of the ages.

Unfortunately, throughout history, people have been tempted to let their hold on God's guidance slip away and to substitute in its place inferior reasoning that is based on human philosophy and the finite logic of the times. Too often, when misguided minds are disconnected from the gentle hints of the Spirit, they wander off on tangents that introduce unfortunate distortions to their understanding of the person and ministry of God. In this book, I'm calling people to reconnect to Scripture, where the light of holy revelation will enable us to see the best path to reverent discovery. Instead of accepting tainted theories, warped heresies, and human opinions that lead nowhere good and certainly not heavenward in praise to God, let us open our minds to the pure Word of God.

This book shows that Scripture offers to the faithful a progressive revelation about the person of God. We have noted the sacred Tetragrammaton, which serves in the Old Testament as the name of the Triune God. We have discovered an inspired pattern in which the men who wrote the Bible refer to God in the singular, while God purposely refers to Himself in plural. And we have seen passages in which God says that He was sent *by God* or *by His Spirit* to do something. Some might consider these riddles and usages to be contradictory—perhaps misinterpretations or textual errors. But that would be to ignore what God wanted His people to understand about Him.

It is the purpose of the New Testament to reveal God through the person of Jesus Christ, the Son. The writers of the various Gospels, epistles, and the book of Revelation followed the example of the Old Testament writers when they named the revered Person of God. And like them, they also avoided speculation regarding the details of the subject of the Godhead and the divine name. We saw an example of that in Christ's charging His disciples to baptize in the *name* (singular) of God, yet including in that name the Father, the Son, and the Holy Spirit. And the man wielding the pen left it at that, without explanations or objections!

There's no doubt about it; the New Testament writers believed that Jesus is God. John, with striking determination, set about giving personal testimony to that fact. He revealed and recapitulated the vision of God as treasured in the Hebrew mind. With deliberation and care, he brought forth in his Gospel the testimony of numerous witnesses, each one helped to fill out a composite picture of Christ, confirming in their own words belief in His divinity. And John himself laid his reputation and his life on the line in defense of Christ's divinity. What greater guarantee could an honorable, truthful apostle of the Lord ever provide than the revelation he had received from above?

The writers of the New Testament ascribed the majestic manifestations of God recorded in the Old Testament to the preincarnate Son of God. As the apostles eventually realized, this very Jesus was personally involved in the great historical works of divine intervention that took place in the time of the patriarchs, prophets, priests, and kings. And while the Old Testament speaks in shadowy figures about a coming "day of the Lord," the New Testament says with unquestionable clarity that the long-hoped-for "day of the Lord" is the promised day of Christ's return.

Scripture, then, provides us with harmonious revelations—though these revelations come recorded in words chosen from the differing vocabularies of a very diverse group of men of God. But when all things have been said and done, each of us must take a very personal step. Will we believe? Will we by faith believe the Word of God? Will we by faith embrace the Savior who is God and who came to earth to reveal the Father?

God is One, there can be no doubt about it. The Old and New Testaments alike support this concept.

To God be the glory for ever and ever!

# Appendix I
# Ellen White on the Trinity

This appendix reviews what Ellen White wrote regarding the Godhead and the harmonious collaboration between God the Father, the Son, and the Holy Spirit. Mrs. White's statements were a key factor in helping the Seventh-day Adventist Church accept the doctrine of the Trinity, her book *The Desire of Ages* being most instrumental in bringing about this change.

## Trinitarian references

"There are three living persons of the heavenly trio; in the name of these three great powers—the Father, the Son, and the Holy Spirit—those who receive Christ by living faith are baptized, and these powers will co-operate with the obedient subjects of heaven in their efforts to live the new life in Christ."—*Special Testimonies,* Series B, no. 7 (1904), 63; also in *Evangelism* (Washington, D.C.: Review and Herald®, 1946), 615.

"As a Christian submits to the solemn rite of baptism, the three highest powers in the universe,—the Father, the Son, and the Holy Spirit,—place their approval on his act, pledging themselves to exert their power in his behalf as he strives to honor God. He is buried in the likeness of Christ's death, and is raised in the likeness of His resurrection. The Saviour went down into the grave, but He rose from the dead, proclaiming over the rent sepulcher, 'I am the Resurrection and the Life.'

"The three great powers of heaven pledge themselves to

furnish the Christian with all the assistance he requires. The Spirit changes the heart of stone to the heart of flesh. And by partaking of the Word of God, Christians obtain an experience that is after the divine similitude. When Christ abides in the heart by faith, the Christian is the temple of God. Christ does not abide in the heart of the sinner, but in the heart of him who is susceptible to the influences of heaven."—"Living for Christ," *Signs of the Times,* August 16, 1905, 9.

"We are baptized in the name of the Father, and of the Son, and of the Holy Ghost, and these three great, infinite powers are unitedly pledged to work in our behalf if we will cooperate with them. We are buried with Christ in baptism as an emblem of His death."—*Lift Him Up* (Hagerstown, Md.: Review and Herald®, 1988), 109.

"As Christians submit to the solemn rite of baptism, He registers the vow that they make to be true to Him. This vow is their oath of allegiance. They are baptized in the name of the Father and the Son and the Holy Spirit. Thus they are united with the three great powers of heaven. They pledge themselves to renounce the world and to observe the laws of the kingdom of God. Henceforth they are to walk in newness of life. No longer are they to follow the traditions of men."—*Evangelism,* 307.

"In the great closing work we shall meet with perplexities that we know not how to deal with, but let us not forget that the three great powers of heaven are working, that a divine hand is on the wheel, and that God will bring His purposes to pass."—*Maranatha* (Washington, D.C.: Review and Herald®, 1976), 252.

"Keep yourselves where the three great powers of heaven—

the Father, the Son, and the Holy Spirit—can be your efficiency. These powers work with the one who gives himself unreservedly to God. The strength of heaven is at the command of God's believing ones. The man who makes God his trust is barricaded by an impregnable wall."—*In Heavenly Places* (Washington, D.C.: Review and Herald®, 1967), 176.

"Clothed with boundless authority, He gave His commission to the disciples: 'Go ye therefore, and teach all nations,' 'baptizing them into the name of the Father and of the Son and of the Holy Spirit: teaching them to observe all things whatsoever I commanded you: and lo, I am with you always, even unto the end of the world.' Matthew 28:19, 20, R. V."—*The Desire of Ages,* 819.

"What a salvation is revealed in the covenant by which God promised to be our Father, His only-begotten Son our Redeemer, and the Holy Spirit our Comforter, Counselor, and Sanctifier! Upon no lower ground than this is it safe for us to place our feet."—*In Heavenly Places,* 137.

"The voice of God calls you as it did Elijah. Come out of the cave and stand with God and hear what He will say unto you. When you will come under the divine guidance, the Comforter will lead you into all truth. The office of the Holy Spirit is to take the things of Christ as they fall from His lips, and infuse them as living principles into the hearts opened to receive them. Then we will know both the Father and the Son."—Letter 40, 1890, 10, 11; also in *Manuscript Releases,* vol. 1 (Silver Spring, Md.: Ellen G. White Estate, 1990), 14:174.

"The ascension of Jesus to the Father was a matter of rejoicing to the early church. It enabled the Saviour to vouchsafe to His followers in a special sense, through the agency of the Holy Spirit, His guidance and protection."—*Manuscript Releases,* vol. 21 (Silver Spring, Md.: Ellen G. White Estate, 1993), 83.

"All who enter into a covenant with Jesus Christ become by adoption the children of God. They are cleansed by the regenerating power of the Word, and angels are commissioned to minister unto them. They are baptized in the name of the Father, of the Son, and of the Holy Ghost. They pledge themselves to become active members of His church in the earth. They are to be dead to all the allurements of worldly desires; but in conversation and godliness, they are, through sanctification of the Spirit to exert a living influence for God."—*Sons and Daughters of God* (Washington, D.C.: Review and Herald®, 1955), 15.

"The Godhead was stirred with pity for the race, and the Father, the Son, and the Holy Spirit gave Themselves to the working out of the plan of redemption. In order fully to carry out this plan, it was decided that Christ, the only-begotten Son of God, should give Himself an offering for sin."—*Counsels on Health* (Mountain View, Calif.: Pacific Press®, 1951), 222.

"The vows which we take upon ourselves in baptism embrace much. In the name of the Father, the Son, and the Holy Spirit we are buried in the likeness of Christ's death and raised in the likeness of His resurrection, and we are to live a new life. Our life is to be bound up with the life of Christ. Henceforth the believer is to bear in mind that he is dedicated to God, to Christ, and to the Holy Spirit."—*Testimonies for the Church* (Mountain View, Calif.: Pacific Press®, 1948), 6:98.

"The Father, the Son, and the Holy Spirit are seeking and longing for channels through which to communicate to the world the divine principles of truth."—*Testimony Treasures* (Mountain View, Calif.: Pacific Press®, 1949), 3:239.

"The fact that you have been baptized in the name of the Father, the Son, and the Holy Spirit is an assurance that, if you will claim Their help, these powers will help you in every emergency."—*Testimony Treasures,* 2:396.

"The work of salvation is not a small matter, but so vast that the highest authorities are taken hold of by the expressed faith of the human agent. The eternal Godhead—the Father, the Son, and the Holy Ghost—is involved in the action required to make assurance to the human agent, . . . confederating the heavenly powers with the human that man may become, through heavenly efficiency, partakers of the divine nature and workers together with Christ."—*The Upward Look* (Washington, D.C.: Review and Herald®, 1982), 148; ellipsis in the original.

"As a Christian submits to the solemn rite of baptism, the three highest powers in the universe—the Father, the Son, and the Holy Spirit—place Their approval on his act, pledging Themselves to exert Their power in his behalf as he strives to honor God."—*Reflecting Christ* (Washington, D.C.: Review and Herald®, 1985), 107.

"Christ has made baptism the sign of entrance to His spiritual kingdom. He has made this a positive condition with which all must comply who wish to be acknowledged as under the authority of the Father, the Son, and the Holy Spirit. Before man can find a home in the church, before passing the threshold of God's spiritual kingdom, he is to receive the impress of the divine name, *'The Lord our Righteousness.'* Jeremiah 23:6.

"Baptism is a most solemn renunciation of the world. Those who are baptized in the threefold name of the Father, the Son, and the Holy Spirit, at the very entrance of their Christian life declare publicly that they have forsaken the service of Satan and have become members of the royal family, children of the heavenly King."—*Testimonies for the Church,* 6:91; emphasis in the original.

"Just before He left them, Christ gave His disciples the promise, 'Ye shall receive power, after that the Holy Ghost is come upon you: and ye shall be witnesses unto Me both in Jerusalem, and in all Judea, and in Samaria, and unto the uttermost part of the earth.' 'Go ye therefore, and teach all nations, baptizing them in the name of the Father, and of the Son, and of the Holy Ghost: teaching them to observe all things whatsoever I have commanded you: and, lo, I am with you always, even unto the end of the world.' While these words were upon His lips, He ascended, a cloud of angels received Him, and escorted Him to the City of God."—*Testimonies to Ministers and Gospel Workers* (Mountain View, Calif.: Pacific Press®, 1944), 65.

"The disciples were to carry their work forward in Christ's name. Their every word and act was to fasten attention on His name, as possessing that vital power by which sinners may be saved. Their faith was to center in Him who is the source of mercy and power. In His name they were to present their petitions to the Father, and they would receive answer. They were to baptize in the name of the Father, the Son, and the Holy Spirit. Christ's name was to be their watchword, their badge of distinction, their bond of union, the authority for their course of action, and the source of their success. Nothing was to be recognized in His kingdom that did not bear His name and superscription."—*The Acts of the Apostles* (Mountain View, Calif.: Pacific Press®, 1911), 28.

## The divinity of Jesus

"The incarnate I AM is our abiding Sacrifice. The I AM is our Redeemer, our Substitute, our Surety. He is the Daysman between God and the human soul, our Advocate in the courts of heaven, our unwearying Intercessor, pleading in our behalf His merits and His atoning sacrifice. The I AM is our Saviour. . . .

"Jehovah is the name given to Christ. 'Behold, God is my salvation,' writes the prophet Isaiah; 'I will trust, and not be afraid; for the Lord JEHOVAH is my strength and my song; He also is become my salvation. Therefore with joy shall ye draw water out of the wells of salvation. And in that day ye shall say, Praise the Lord, call upon His name, declare His doings among the people, make mention that His name is exalted.' 'In that day shall this song be sung in the land of Judah: We have a strong city; salvation will God appoint for walls and bulwarks. Open ye the gates, that the righteous nation which keepeth the truth may enter in. Thou wilt keep him in perfect peace whose mind is stayed on Thee, because he trusted in Thee. Trust ye in the Lord forever, for in the Lord JEHOVAH is everlasting strength.' "— "The Word Made Flesh," *Signs of the Times,* May 3, 1899, 2.

"The apostles, instead of being sad, disheartened, and discouraged, ready to yield up their faith in Christ, full of courage, proclaiming, by the power of the Holy Spirit, the divinity of Christ. They hear them declare with boldness that the Man recently humiliated, spit upon, derided, smitten by cruel hands, crowned with thorns, and crucified, is the Prince of Life, and that He is now sitting at the right hand of God."—"The Promise of the Spirit," *Signs of the Times,* May 17, 1899, 2.

## About the Holy Spirit

"We need to realize that the Holy Spirit, who is as much a person as God is a person, is walking through these grounds."—Manuscript 66, 1899, from a talk to the students at the Avondale school; also in *Evangelism,* 616.

"The Holy Spirit is a person, for He beareth witness with our spirits that we are the children of God. When this witness is borne, it carries with it its own evidence. At such times we believe and are sure that we are the children of God. . . .

"The Holy Spirit has a personality, else He could not bear witness to our spirits and with our spirits that we are the children of God. He must also be a divine person, else He could not search out the secrets which lie hidden in the mind of God. 'For what man knoweth the things of a man, save the spirit of man which is in him? even so the things of God knoweth no man, but the Spirit of God.' "—Manuscript 20, 1906; also in *Evangelism,* 616, 617; ellipses in original.

"The Holy Spirit was the highest of all gifts that He [Jesus] could solicit from His Father for the exaltation of His people. The Spirit was to be given as a regenerating agent, and without this the sacrifice of Christ would have been of no avail. The power of evil had been strengthening for centuries, and the submission of men to this satanic captivity was amazing. Sin could be resisted and overcome only through the mighty agency of the third person of the Godhead, who would come with no modified energy, but in the fullness of divine power."—*The Faith I Live By* (Washington, D.C.: Review and Herald®, 1958), 52.

"What saith our Saviour? 'I will not leave you comfortless: I will come to you.' 'He that hath my commandments, and keepeth them, he it is that loveth me: and he that loveth me shall be loved of my Father; and I will love him, and will manifest myself to him.' When trials overshadow the soul, remember the words of Christ, remember that He is an unseen presence in the person of the Holy Spirit, and He will be the peace and comfort given you, manifesting to you that He is with you, the Sun of Righteousness, chasing away your darkness. 'If a man love me,' Christ said, 'he will keep my words: and my Father will love him, and we will come unto him, and make our abode with him.' Be of good cheer; light will come, and your soul will rejoice greatly in the Lord."—Letter 124, 1897; also in *Daughters of God* (Hagerstown, Md.: Review and Herald®, 1998), 185.

# Some Documentary Evidence, 1862–1932

This appendix provides a glimpse of the attitude of the church and of some of its early leaders toward the doctrine of the Trinity, with references and Internet addresses (in the endnotes) so interested readers can look at photocopies of the originals at the Web site provided by the Office of Archives and Statistics of the General Conference of Seventh-day Adventists.

## Evidence 1: The baptismal formula

One of the complexities of this topic stems from the fact that while some of the pioneers denied the Trinity in concept, they did use the Trinitarian formula when they performed baptisms. In an article titled "Perpetuity of Spiritual Gifts" that James White wrote for the *Review and Herald,* he explained why, "Baptism is a perpetual ordinance in the church, and the ministers of the nineteenth century [the current century when he wrote this article] baptize 'in the name of the Father, and of the Son, and of the Holy Ghost' because the original commission requires it."[1]

## Evidence 2: An anti-Trinitarian editor's answer

The editor of the *Review and Herald* was responsible for the section of questions and answers titled "In the Question Chair." When Uriah Smith was the editor of the *Review and Herald,* a reader sent in a question regarding the "baptism for the dead" that Paul mentioned in 1 Corinthians 15:19. Smith was not a Trinitarian; however, his answer to the question (presuming he was the one who answered it) includes this sentence: "The formula given for baptism is, 'In the name of the Father, and of the Son, and of the Holy Ghost.' Matt. 28:19."[2]

## Evidence 3: A pioneer's sermon

In a sermon preached by Stephen N. Haskell, which was printed in the *Review and Herald* two months later, he said, "We believe in baptism, and we have the same formula as the Baptists. Both baptize in the name of the Father and of the Son and of the Holy Ghost."[3]

## Evidence 4: A direct reference to the Trinity

An issue of the *Review and Herald* published in 1913 (just two years before Ellen White's death), when Francis M. Wilcox was the general editor and Charles M. Snow and William Spicer were assistant editors, contained an article titled "The Message for Today." This piece, written by the editor, makes the following statement:

> For the benefit of those who may desire to know more particularly the cardinal features of the faith held by this denomination, we shall state that Seventh-day Adventists believe,—
>
> 1. In the divine Trinity. This Trinity consists of the eternal Father, a personal, spiritual being, omnipotent, omniscient, infinite in power, wisdom, and love; of the Lord Jesus Christ, the Son of the eternal Father, through whom all things were created, and through whom the salvation of the redeemed host will be accomplished; the Holy Spirit, the third

person of the Godhead, the one regenerating agency
in the work of redemption.[4]

## Evidence 5: The official Adventist position in 1932

Section 11 of the *Church Manual* published by the General Conference of Seventh-day Adventists in 1932 is a statement of the fundamental beliefs of the church. The second and third beliefs listed there are germane to our topic, the Trinity. They read as follows:

> 2. That the Godhead, or Trinity, consists of the Eternal Father, a personal, spiritual Being, omnipotent, omnipresent, omniscient, infinite in wisdom and love; the Lord Jesus Christ, the Son of the Eternal Father, through whom all things were created and through whom the salvation of the redeemed hosts will be accomplished; the Holy Spirit, the third person of the Godhead, the great regenerating power in the work of redemption. Matt. 28:19.
>
> 3. That Jesus Christ is very God, being of the same nature and essence as the Eternal Father. While retaining His divine nature, He took upon Himself the nature of the human family, lived on earth as a man, exemplified in His life as our example the principles of righteousness, attested His relationship to God by many mighty miracles, died for our sins on the cross, was raised from the dead, and ascended to the Father, where He ever lives to make intercession for us. John 1:1, 14; Heb. 2:9-18; 8:1, 2; 4:14-16; 7:25.[5]

1. James White, "Perpetuity of Spiritual Gifts," *Review and Herald,* February 4, 1862, 76, http://www.adventistarchives.org/doc_info .asp?DocID=88702.

2. Uriah Smith [?], "850.—Baptized for the Dead," *Review and Herald,* January 21, 1902, 42, http://www.adventistarchives.org/doc_info .asp?DocID=92218.

3. Stephen N. Haskell, "The Sanctuary," *Review and Herald,* November 3, 1904, 8, http://www.adventistarchives.org/doc_info .asp?DocID=91738. This article was from a sermon he preached in College View, Nebraska, on September 17, 1904.

4. Francis M. Wilcox, "The Message for Today," *Review and Herald,* October 9, 1913, 21, http://www.adventistarchives.org/doc_info .asp?DocID=90995.

5. General Conference of Seventh-day Adventists, *Church Manual* (n.p.: The General Conference of Seventh-day Adventists, 1932), 180, http://www.adventistarchives.org/doc_info.asp?DocID=119305.